Although the path for each person is different, there are certain truths that are common for all paths. Manifestation is one of these truths. There is no lack in the Universe. Whether seeking prosperity or love, there is an unlimited supply for all. Limitations exist only in the mind, yet can keep prosperity and love from appearing in the physical. When you transcend these limitations and learn to trust in yourself and the universe, then you have true freedom.

– Sananda –

Manifesting Your Heart's Desire
Book II

Fred Fengler
Todd Varnum

Heartlight Publishing

An earlier version of this book was published in 1996
with the title
Opening to Your Higher Self.
ISBN 0-9641305-1-3
An epilogue has been added to bring the reader up to
date with some of the personal examples shared in
this book.

Published by HeartLight Publishing

ISBN 0-9641305-3-X

Cover Design by Steve Redmond
Book Design by Mark Wanner
Edited by Annie DiSpirito

Contents

Manifesting Your Heart's Desire
Book II

Chapter 1

We Create Everything in Our Life: So We Are Told

Universal Intelligence: You are *all* powerful beings. *You* are capable of creating anything you wish. When you set into motion those things that you want through the power of your conscious thoughts the entire universe goes to work to bring you what you desire.

Me: You mean I can create a new car for myself? A better job? A wonderful romantic relationship?

Universal Intelligence: Absolutely! All you need to do is to be clear and consistent in your desire. It is also important to recognize and neutralize any counteracting beliefs, and influences or habits, that might not be in harmony with your intended creation. Be sure that your intent to have a new car is accompanied by the thought that you deserve it and can afford it. Feel the joy of having it in this moment.

Me: That's incredible! But what happens when I'm not concentrating on having something? Are my thoughts creating all the time?

Universal Intelligence: Of course, they are. There is nothing in your life you have not created; although there are some things that you create cooperatively with others. You cannot be made to do anything without your permission. And, you cannot make someone else do anything without their cooperation and permission. Of course, much of this goes on beyond your conscious awareness. For instance, a car dealer is preparing your car for you right now even though you and she have not yet met each other.

Me: Wow! So, yesterday, when I ran into a very good friend I'd been trying to reach—that was no accident? And, when I happened to be at the box office for a sold out concert just as two people returned tickets, I was being guided by some intelligence? Now that I think about it, it did seem more than coincidence both times.

Universal Intelligence: Of course it was. *You* created those situations. In each case, you had a clear intent without a great deal of attachment to the outcome. The universe went to work to support you.

Me: You know, this really does make sense. I never realized I had so much creative power. But, wait a minute! Last month, I was in a serious automobile accident. On my last trip to New York City, I was assaulted and robbed. And, I'm just getting over this bout with pneumonia. Are you saying I created these things, too?

Universal Intelligence: You certainly did! Remember, you create *everything* in your life. How many of the events you participate in, or people who daily cross your path, are chosen by you?

Me: I have no idea.

Universal Intelligence: All of them! No exceptions!

Me: Oh, come on! Why would I want to be robbed, or injured, or sick? I can't accept that!

Universal Intelligence: Not on a conscious level, perhaps. Until now, you have never allowed yourself to be aware of how your consciousness works *for* you. If you don't wish to create these things in your life, you must become aware. Only *you* can decide if you are ready to learn how your thoughts work for you.

Me: I am willing to start, but I'm still skeptical. Is that OK?

Universal Intelligence It sure is. Be skeptical. Your own experience will be your best teacher.

In our previous book, *Manifesting Your Heart's Desire*, we explored the relationship between our conscious beliefs and the physically manifested outcomes that followed. We coordinated a group, which met regularly for several years, and began by experimenting with items or experiences, like manifesting parking places, where little attachment was involved.

As we developed confidence in our abilities, we took on bigger challenges, such as desirable relationships and rewarding jobs. These larger challenges usually brought up undermining beliefs and strong attachments to outcomes, which resulted in longer delays between the desire and its manifestation. For example, on a conscious level we might be trying to manifest economic abundance in our lives, but, a deep seated belief in scarcity or unworthiness on a subconscious level prevents us from receiving that abundance. As a result, we tend to manifest experiences in our lives from both conscious and unconscious sources.

But, there was a third kind of experience we were manifesting which was not the result of either a conscious desire, or a subconscious belief. How could we account for the presence of illnesses, accidents, or criminal acts committed against us? Some people seemed to have a great deal of so-called bad luck. Perhaps they were always in the wrong place at the wrong time.

We also wondered how manifesting could account for the reason materializing money was so easy for some, yet so difficult for others. On the other hand, why were those materially well-off having difficulty manifesting a healthy relationship, while those who had little income had a relationship we all admired? Others with satisfying jobs, as well as satisfying relationships, seemed to have endless health problems.

Although some of these situations might be explained by unconscious beliefs which accounted for the undesirable manifestation, this explanation was not convincing for many of the group members. Why, we asked, would someone create a fatal illness or an auto accident? There seemed to be a whole class of experiences in our lives that could not be accounted for by either our conscious manifestations of the first kind, or our unconscious manifestations of the second kind.

The group members, as they continued to share manifestations with each other beyond the first year, found their awareness expanding to another level of consciousness and learning. Some sensed that their daily experiences were part of a much larger plan. If an individual could tune in to the flow of life's experiences, he or she seemed to live in greater harmony and happiness. This flow of what unfolded in life appeared to originate from the higher superconscious part of the self which was the seat of this larger plan.

Others of us weren't sure we could identify this intuitive sensing, nor were we willing to trust it at first. This expanded consciousness, or awareness, of this plan usually did not occur until some time had passed in our manifesting experimentation.

Channeled Guidance

Group members found the information received from three channeled entities very helpful. These entities called themselves Sir Garrod, McDermott, and Sananda. They clarified for us why certain experiences appeared in our life. They also supported, empowered, and encouraged us when we felt lost and helpless. For many of us, these spiritual teachers appeared to have access to information from a "higher" consciousness, or oversoul, which provides us with valuable insight and can assist us in making choices in our present circumstances.

We kept detailed records of their information via taping and transcribing sessions for a period of ten years. During this period, a camaraderie and mutual respect grew between the entities and ourselves.

The entities said if we could see them, it would be as beings of light or energy, as opposed to having physical forms. Since consciousness is greatly expanded in the spiritual dimension, they see the larger whole of ourselves, of which our physical selves are a small though significant part. According to Sir Garrod, human consciousness was deliberately focused, so that souls could learn in ways difficult to achieve in the spiritual dimension. Therefore, learning in the physical realm is important, and should not be judged as being of less merit or value simply because we are not presently in spiritual form.

They also said that neither personal names, nor gender, have any meaning in their dimension. Spiritual beings are both male and female; the duality of sex or gender experienced in our dimension is part of the illusion we are exploring. Channeled entities take personal names for convenience in human communication. Although there is a sense of individuality in their plane of existence, names are truly meaningless in the spiritual dimension.

We became increasingly aware of the difficulties that Sir Garrod, McDermott, and Sananda have when communicating with us. Not only were we suspicious of some of this spiritual information, but the entities need to use a language based on our physical reality. A comparable challenge for humans might be if an isolated stone age culture were discovered in a remote area of the world. What words or metaphors could we use to communicate the significance of twentieth century technology? How would we explain to them about television, airplanes, and missiles?

We, the authors, attempted to put ourselves in the place of a spirit entity trying to communicate to us as humans, who were living in, and only comfortable with a tangible three dimensional world. We were told that we perceive our experiences through an extremely focused and limited consciousness. If positions were reversed, how would we communicate with a being who considered space, time, and cause and effect as absolutely real conditions, and found it impossible, unimaginable, and threatening to conceive life outside these parameters?

We were told we are actors living out a script we had written for ourselves. We then forgot we had authored the script and had the power to rewrite it. We were convinced that the roles we play encompass our existence.

At first, this concept was astounding. But, thinking back to a book we read years before, called *Flatland*, we drew some parallels with our position. Although we could not remember the exact details, we recalled that the story dealt with the fictitious world of two dimensional objects, like circles, squares, and triangles. It was a reality in which spheres, cubes, and pyramids did not exist.

One night, the main character, a circle, has a disturbing dream in which he visits Lineland, a one dimensional realm whose inhabitants can only move from point to point. He tries to explain that he is from a realm where you can move not only from point to point, but from side to side, and can change directions so that a circle, such as he, is formed. The angry Linelanders are about to attack him when he awakens.

A few days later, the same circle encounters a sphere passing through his plane of reality. To us, it would be like passing a ball through a glass plate. It appeared to the circle as a dot appearing out of nowhere, like a ghost. This, in itself, was astonishing, but, to his further amazement, it grew into a circle. Circle asks the ghost, "Who are you? Where do you come from?"

The ghost answers by saying simply, "I am a sphere. I exist in three dimensions. You are living in a two-dimensional world, which to you seems real. You think the two-dimensional world is all that is real. You can't see the third dimension, but it exists!" With that, the sphere bids good day, and, to the further amazement of the circle, shrinks to a dot. Before his very eyes, the sphere disappears.

Circle was so excited, he couldn't wait to tell his friends. One friend scoffed at him, and said, "You are seeing things. This can't be true. Everyone knows there can't be a third dimension." Even Circle's best friend said, "I don't know whether what you saw is a hallucination or not, but, as your best friend, I would advise you not to mention it. It is upsetting to people."

When we first began working with McDermott, Sananda and Sir Garrod, we were skeptical about the source of their information. Working with these entities over several years convinced us, that, regardless of the source, the knowledge was helpful to us during our learning process. We saw how their insights and interpretations for other members of the group, and even strangers, were both helpful and accurate. In addition, we gained insight into a spiritual world that contained parameters and processes which we found not only awesome and wondrous, but consistent with all that we were learning from our study of quantum physics. Science and spirituality were not as dichotomous as we were first led to believe.

While we were not able to confirm all the information we were receiving, there was a strong knowing about what we were learning. Again and again, the information made sense on a deep soul level. The entities always encouraged us to retain a healthy skepticism; which we did. Most of the time, we met with them separately, and grew to appreciate three individuals with different, but usually complementary, perspectives. Because we were using different entities with somewhat different frames of reference on reality, it was easier to retain our open skepticism. We also read widely the messages of many other channeled entities, which showed surprising consistency with the information we received from Sir Garrod, Sananda and McDermott.

When people asked us whether they should take seriously all they were told by the entities, we told them what we always told ourselves: take what is useful and either discard, or place off to the side, the rest. Ultimately, the responsibility for all our experiences, and the interpretation of those experiences, rests with us.

These entities did not want to be revered as all-knowing deities. In fact, they wished for us to be self-reliant and able to access information for ourselves by getting in touch with our inner guides and using our intuition.

Prior to working with the new perspectives, we demonstrated that we consciously have the power to create our own realities. We also learned how our unconscious beliefs manifest. We could enhance our manifesting power to the extent we became aware of those unconscious beliefs. The channeled entities added a framework to help us interpret our experiences on a broader basis. Manifesting is part of a larger process of learning tied in with our life purpose.

At first, the information the channeled entities gave us seemed quite wild and improbable. But, as we worked within their framework, it helped us understand that a lot of experiences we were having couldn't be explained as either a result of conscious manifesting, nor as a result of less conscious beliefs.

They said that when we think of who we are, we tend to think of ourselves as a conscious entity who makes choices, and experiences material life with five senses. However, there is another part of us we do not see which is our higher self. Our higher self is not "higher" because it is better. It is higher because it possesses a broader perspective. This concept can be compared to standing on top of a mountain and looking down into the valley, compared with standing on the valley floor. From the mountain top, the forest is seen as a whole, while in the valley, the view is much narrower, and only individual trees are recognized.

We were told that before we enter physical existence we establish a plan, or purpose, for our life. We choose, in general, to learn certain lessons during our physical incarnation. We also designate the context in which we learn those lessons. We select a certain culture, social class, and set of parents which will facilitate our learning. These choices serve to create certain energy patterns in our lives that attract to us events, people, and situations during our lifetime that advance our purpose.

Although the plan is set into motion before we incarnate, it is purposely forgotten by our physical selves because the

lessons are more powerful if we don't remember we created
them. Sir Garrod, Sananda, and McDermott emphasized that
events are more real, and learning more accelerated, when
we don't remember our true spiritual nature and origin. Like
a horse with blinders, we can no longer see the larger context of which we are a part. We can only experience a very
narrow linear portion of existence. But, blinders allow us to
focus on living in physical reality.

As a soul, you create the stage and the plot of the play.
At that point you split into your spiritual consciousness,
and your physical self. The spiritual portion of you retains
awareness of your purpose and the play, while your physical portion becomes the actor who interprets the role. The
actor exists on a vast stage with roles to perform, but he
has forgotten it is only a stage. It is not that the play has
been completed in advance, for we consciously participate
in writing our scripts from moment to moment because we
are constantly making choices.

We tend to forget that we are the writers, directors, and
stars in our own larger drama. That information resides
beyond our consciousness within our higher self. Even
though separated into conscious and less-conscious seg-
ments, there is constant interaction between the two com-
ponents of the self. The higher self will continually bring to
us appropriate situations that help us follow our plan, even
though the physical self may not be aware the situations
are learning opportunities instead of hardships.

Another way to view our lives as physical beings, is to
envision ourselves as students in the big classroom of life,
enrolled in a preselected course with a great deal of choice in
how we learn the course material. An analogy is the student
who chooses a major course of study, and each semester is
presented with the courses needed to master the subject matter. The experiences we create during our waking state are

designed to help us learn those pre-chosen lessons. We may incarnate over and over again while we learn those lessons, often with an infinite number of variations attached.

Moreover, the plan is flexible; nothing is set in concrete. We may learn our lessons with a fair degree of conscious- ness, and without a great deal of drama. If we don't learn them with minimal drama, we may find our higher self creating more dramatic situations to get our attention. We may repeat the situations over and over again until we learn the lessons. We may even choose to ignore our purpose and postpone the lessons until another lifetime. And, we may add lessons to our curriculum after incarnating.

Finally, all our lessons are coordinated with other people, and we will be attracted to those others who will facilitate our learning process and their own as well. Our individual plans were linked with everyone else's, with a sense of interconnectedness and perfection that we could only glimpse. We simultaneously facilitated everyone else's plan when we followed our own.

This plan for lessons, decided on before incarnating in human form, helped us understand why we attracted cer- tain people, situations, and experiences into our lives. This "third kind" of manifesting came not from our conscious de- sires, nor our unconscious beliefs, but from our higher self, which we could learn to access. All of our experiences could be traced to one of these three processes of manifesting.

With the advent of this new, expanded, perspective with which to view the manifestation process, we felt that a sec- ond book was needed. Our first book, *Manifesting Your Heart's Desire*, emphasized the appreciation of our own in- dividual power, and the ability to realize goals and desires. In this second book, we concentrate on manifestations of the third kind, and the emphasis is more on the process and appreciation of the larger meaning derived from our lesson plan. Some situations and experiences seemed unrelated to any apparent desired goal. Other experiences, over time, can be appreciated as part of a larger process of learning designed to attain the goal. Many of our larger goals manifested over long periods of time, with attendant experiences and lessons connected with our lesson plan. For example, we can learn a lot about ourselves while trying to manifest a wonderful job or relationship.

Instead of manifesting remaining an occasional activity using conscious goals, and methods for the attainment of those goals, manifesting became a *process* that existed in every moment of every day. The desired goal may serve as the incentive, but the significance often lay in the situations encountered on the way to the goal. Manifesting of all three kinds became a way of life, a wondrous, though often puzzling, unfolding of events and experiences tied in with beliefs both conscious and unconscious, and linked to an enormous plan of learning.

Working with McDermott, Sananda and Sir Garrod over several years, we derived seven basic principles to use as models for perceiving our life experiences. We decided to use our life experiences to test this set of principles.

These seven principles were drawn from teachings given to us by the channeled entities to "wear" for a period of time. How well did these principles explain what was going on in our lives, and with what consequences? Did the quality of our life change? If so, how? Since many of these principles were quite different from the way we had previously envisioned our lives, we were also interested to see how they related to our present experiences.

We decided to directly test these theories by using our daily experiences as data. The ideas which the channeled entities presented to us were intriguing, but, did they work? Would our lives become more meaningful or enjoyable as we played with these interpretations of daily events? We just didn't know. But we did know we couldn't find the answers by merely talking about these new philosophies with the channeled entities, or debating among ourselves in an abstract intellectual forum.

Although not intended as a set of formal scientific hypotheses the principles did provide a common foundation for investigation. They were designed to serve as guidelines as we explored and evaluated the meaningfulness and usefulness of this broader spiritual explanation of how and why we have certain experiences in our lives.

The Seven Principles

ONE: All Life Forms Are Interconnected

The experiences that unfold for us are intricately interconnected with the experiences of growth and learning of all other individuals with which we interact, although our consciousness limits our awareness of this seemingly complex process.

Beneath the diversity of physical life forms is an energy of unity connecting with these forms. Not only does this allow us to communicate with each other on a telepathic frequency, but, also, it is possible for us to communicate with animals and plants. Many of us have that type of rapport with our pets; others feel they can communicate with plants, as well. There is a vast intricately connected network of energies beyond anything the human mind can comprehend.

TWO: We Are Connected to a Higher Intelligence

For the moment, assume that behind these intricately interconnected patterns of energy is an intelligence that is beyond our conscious waking self and our less-conscious belief systems. This intelligence can have many names, such as oversoul, or cosmic force, or God, or higher self. We prefer to use higher self, because it is defined as something beyond our conscious self, yet still a part of our identity. This higher self is constantly interacting with our consciousness and creating experiences for us. Even though it may be difficult for us to comprehend the meanings of, or reasons for, some events in our lives, there is a benevolent intelligence, our higher self, creating the experiences for our own growth and learning.

Although, when describing our higher self, it may appear to be separate from us, it is still our self—only in a different state of expanded consciousness. An analogy is when we are deeply absorbed in an activity, such as playing tennis. We may become so intensely focused on the game, or the point at hand, that for a short time we block out our awareness of everything else. Nothing else matters while we are playing that point. After the point has been played, our awareness expands to include realization that our body needs water, our opponent needs to be complimented on a good play, it is time to go back to work, etc. Perhaps our present lifetime, from another perspective, would be viewed as one focused point in a long tennis match.

THREE: Intuition Links Us to Our Higher Intelligence

We have the ability to access the intelligence of the higher self. We can learn how to expand our consciousness and, at least in part, increase awareness and meaning about the experiences we are attracting into our lives. This means discovering how to make decisions and choices based on their alignment with our higher purpose. This intelligence is also available to show us the meaning behind the experiences we create for ourselves.

Most of us already tune in to this intelligence whenever we employ intuition in our daily lives. Sometimes we refer to it as following a hunch, or having a gut reaction. We can train ourselves to pay attention to this source of guidance, and observe what happens when we do, and don't, listen. Stop before making a decision and ask yourself for a sense of what you should do, then notice how you *feel*; your body sensations, thoughts, and/or emotions. We can teach ourselves to distinguish between true intuition and decision making which uses reasoning while paying attention to mind chatter.

FOUR: We Create, and Are Responsible For, All Our Experiences

One of the more difficult principles to accept is that we create everything in our lives. We are individually responsible for everything that happens to us. We are never victims of external circumstances. It does not matter whether the experiences are consciously caused, unconsciously motivated, or derived from the higher self. Nor does it matter whether the experience is perceived to be good or bad; fortunate or unfortunate. Fate, chance, or luck are never factors used to account for our life experiences. We create, or co-create with others, all events in our lives.

FIVE: All Life Forms Are Engaged in Mutual Learning

All of us have chosen certain experiences, understandings, and lessons to explore while in physical form. Some of our learning is personal; relating to our own growth process. Other aspects may be linked with those in our immediate circle of family and friends. Still others may be part of large groups, even those which are global in scope. Furthermore, not only are we manifesting moment to moment our desires, beliefs, and experiences around lessons from our higher selves but these manifestations are simultaneously coordinated with everyone else's desires, beliefs, and lessons.

A person may have chosen to learn about the power of the mind to heal the body. By so doing, she may find herself attracting healers who assist her in transcending the medical diagnosis of a terminal illness. In a complimentary fashion, the healers have attracted people who need healing so they can develop their skills. Ultimately, according to McDermott, if everyone followed internal guidance for self expression and decision making, the result would be a vast, harmonious, societal web of joyous individuals doing what they love and in mutual support of each other.

SIX: There Are No Accidents

As a consequence of the previous principle that we create everything, experiences and events in our everyday life are never the product of chance. All of the situations and people we encounter are the result of one, or more, of the three types of manifesting. There are conscious patterns which are easily explained because of our individual choices, participation in certain institutions, a larger culture, and society. Growing up in a family that is abusive or loving, or within a culture that is technologically advanced or primitive, can greatly influence how we view the world, the individual experiences we attract, and the choices we make. Many social scientists devote their research to explaining how our personal, historical, and environmental circumstances shape our world view.

Sometimes we have an experience that cannot be easily explained, but we intuitively know it is more than coincidence. For example, perhaps you were just thinking of some-one you hadn't thought of in a long time. A few minutes later you receive a phone call or a letter from that person. Although you cannot account for this particular sequence of events in a causal way, you just know they are connected. It is not mere coincidence.

SEVEN: We Always Have the Choice of How to Respond to Experience

It is important to recognize that we are not puppets ruled, or manipulated, by our higher selves. There is always a choice of how we wish to respond to experiences or mes-sages that we create in conjunction with, or receive from, our higher self. Through intuition, we may choose to judge our experiences any way we wish, and usually do, based on our beliefs, past experiences, or perceived needs. A rainy day may be judged quite differently by a foreign tourist with a list of outdoor sights to visit, compared with a local farmer suffering through a prolonged drought.

Learning to listen and flow with the inner voice, or link with our higher self, may seem to be an obvious choice. But, there also may be times when we choose not to listen. And, when we do so, that choice is not to be judged as being in-correct. Every situation presents choices to us for learning and there are many ways to learn.

A person's intuition may be guiding them to quit their present job and relocate to another area and other employ-ment. However, they may experience extreme guilt over how negatively this might affect their family, or be filled with so much fear that they would be unable to start over, they de-cide that making the change would not be worth the risk. Like this person, we are always free to make our own choice.

In other situations, our higher self may intensify the experiences for us if we choose not to pay attention to smaller, less dramatic, events. These are presented to us to keep us focused on our lessons. But, again, in all these situations, we have choices of how to respond, including ignoring our chosen lessons.

This entire book and all the incidents, our own and others, that we present and examine, is designed to explore the seven principles. We are also motivated by the question, "so what?" We are curious to know how our lives, and the lives of others who follow this spiritual perspective toward life, have changed.

We begin by examining the significance of interconnectedness to help us understand how, and why, we are able to do manifestations of the first kind. We also explore how our less conscious beliefs serve to enhance, or limit, our abilities to manifest what we desire.

We follow with our first look at the role manifestations of the third kind plays in our lives. There are simply too many experiences that can not be accounted for by recognition of the role of conscious manifesting, or through awareness of our less-conscious beliefs.

Our method is to examine events from our past using the seven principles. How well does this cosmic, or spiritual, paradigm fit earlier periods of our lives? In retrospect, can we now discover meaning and purpose to events which we could not see at the time they unfolded?

We then turn to incidents and experiences in our everyday lives. How can these principles help us with decision making, as well as perceiving events from moment to moment? How is the knowledge useful to us when we assume that everything that happens to us, from a car that breaks down to a sold out concert, is part of some higher learning experience?

Finally, we turn to those experiences when it is most difficult to choose not to be a victim. Would one supposedly create a life-long, chronic disability for some higher learning purpose? Surely, logic tells us, we do not create a life-threatening illness to grow and become enlightened. Yet, we have assumed, as part of our investigation and as one of our basic principles, that all experiences are self-created for our own growth and learning.

It is not necessary to be consistent and accept all seven of the principles. Our culture tends to put a high premium on consistency, and an all-or-nothing acceptance of belief systems.

We tend to see ourselves as a bridge between two worlds. What is presented in the following chapters is what we, and the group members, have found through testing this model of spiritual principles by using our own experiences. The reader is then free to choose whether they wish to "try on" any or all of the seven spiritual principles for themselves, and see how they fit (or don't fit) into their life.

Chapter 2

The Web of Interconnectedness

In *Manifesting Your Heart's Desire Book I*, the focus was on manifestations of the first and second kind. We were interested in how to create what we consciously desired, and to recognize how our less conscious beliefs manifested in our lives.

While greatly enjoying this new tool of self empowerment, we also became curious about how we were able to create what we wanted. How was it possible that a desire for an experience or an object would manifest through what, on the surface, might be perceived as a rather amazing series of "coincidental" events?

If this was more than chance, then what type of a communication system was operating to bring about the desired experience, often in ways that could not be anticipated beforehand? Was there a massive computer in the heavens intricately linking everyone's conscious thoughts, desires, and beliefs with the necessary people and events to ensure coordination of the results? For example, a desire for a parking place is linked through thought energy with someone's readiness to make their space available. How common is it to have the feeling of being linked with another in our conscious state? Almost everyone has experienced thinking of someone, and having them call.

A member of the manifestation group bought a locally published book to send to his mother. She wanted to send it to a friend as a gift. He told her to expect to receive it soon. However, a series of incidents delayed it being sent through the mail.

"My wife and I were waiting for several things to fall into place so we could do them all together including the mailing of the gift. I could feel myself becoming increasingly anxious. I told my wife we had to get it out right away. I found myself tuning into my mother, and could feel her nervousness. I continued to pick up her concern and realized the perfect moment for mailing was not going to arrive. I had to get the book out right away!

"The day after I mailed it I awoke, again feeling my mother's apprehension. I just knew she would call. I decided to call her. She confirmed she was just going to telephone me. She said she started becoming anxious three days before, the same time I began worrying about sending the gift. I told her I had mailed it to her. I just know I was telepathically picking up on her anxiety."

What is this energy that connects all of us, and, can it be measured? If it can't be measured, can its effects be documented more scientifically than by simply relying on anecdotal incidents?

Larry Dossey, in his book *Healing Words*, and other researchers have been reporting and investigating the power of prayer to heal at a distance. Patients who were prayed for, even over long distances, were compared with patients with similar healing needs but who were not prayed for. On many different measures, the group prayed for healed much more rapidly and completely. What was the link between the person doing the praying, and the patient who was the recipient of the prayer?

Scientific research has demonstrated that if groups of individuals engage in the practice of transcendental meditation, the stress level of an entire community can be reduced, including those who do not practice meditation. This shows up in a variety of statistics, such as a reduction in the crime rate when a certain proportion of residents of a community meditate over a period of time. This phenomenon is referred to as the Maharashi Effect. It assumes we are all participants in a collective social consciousness that can be influenced through meditation, resulting in a more harmonious and coherent social environment.

Physicists who study the smallest building blocks of matter suggest there is another dimension of existence; a deeper level of reality beyond the material and the objective, where separateness vanishes, and all things appear to be part of an unbroken whole. Out of this basic foundation of interconnectedness arises a dimension where particles appear separate and, in turn, form the level of reality of which we, as humans, are consciously aware.

Sir Garrod pointed out that beyond the subatomic level, we are all made up of the same God energy. This energy can take many forms. The analogy he used was water, a common substance able to take many forms, but is still the same material. Sir Garrod states, "An Eskimo sitting on a glacier boiling water is surrounded by ice, water, vapor, clouds; all different forms of the same substance. Even the Eskimo's body is two thirds water."

In the human state we tend to feel separation and exaggerate the differences between us. "As a person living in ordinary waking consciousness, you tend to see a world dominated by differences and fragments." Sir Garrod continues, "On the other hand, a person experiencing an expanded consciousness sees the fragments, but also sees, underneath the differences, patterns of connectedness and meaning. Everything is organically connected with everything else and shares a common underlying field of origin. Simply put, underneath all diversity is unity."

Like Flatlanders trying to comprehend a three dimensional existence, so do those of us living in an existence of time, space, and separation, have difficulty comprehending a dimension where distinct forms or objects disappear and are replaced by a seamless web of interconnected energies transcending time and space. Yet, interestingly to us, this description by modern physicists of the quantum world turned out to be quite similar to Sir Garrod's description of the spiritual dimension.

According to Sir Garrod, our true state outside of our physical body is one of incredible interconnectedness, which still allows us to retain our individual identity. The separated state we experience in physical form is a very unnatural state. But, this material state allows us to focus, so that we can have certain experiences and lessons only possible in this type of environment. We chose to be part of one big experiment where we live under the illusion that we are solid and separate entities.

We deliberately reduced and focused our consciousness so we can explore what it is like to live in an environment where being separate seemed real. Our spiritual state is quite different and exists in a state of interconnectedness with everything. Beneath our conscious awareness is the memory of our true state as interconnected energy beings. Moreover, not only are we interconnected as humans, but all matter is interconnected as part of a vast, functioning network of interacting parts.

Referring to manifesting a parking place, the person sent out a mental radar energy scanning for people who would be leaving when he was scheduled to arrive at a particular destination. Perhaps he found all the lights turning green on the way to the desired location, or all the lights turning red to delay him, so the spot would be vacant as he arrived. Underneath all the diversity of people, animals, plants, and objects was a common unifying energy connecting all these seemingly discrete entities with each other.

Using this principle of interconnectedness, could it help us explain the way our desired experiences unfold? This could not be proved in a scientific sense, but did it serve to explain how we were able to manifest what we consciously desired? The members of the manifestation group found this information helpful in explaining experiences in their daily life.

Manifestation Group Members' Experiences

"It always amazes me how the universe brings to me what I need," said Annie. "Over the weekend I saw an ad for a concert and said, 'Gee, I would like to go to that,' and the next thing Heather calls me up with tickets and asks, 'Do you want to go?' We went, and I really enjoyed it. A few days later I saw an ad for a movie and said, 'That looks like a fun movie. I wish I could go.' A friend called up and gave me a free ticket for the movie. I was also out of food, but had not mentioned it to anyone, and she brought me a big bag of vegetables from her garden when she brought the ticket. I found that when I need help, the person who can help shows up. I am also learning to appreciate gifts without the feeling of guilt."

Jill said she had noticed ongoing manifestations happening almost daily in her life. She remarked that it always seemed to be like a lottery to get the shuttle bus from the parking lot to campus, a half-mile away. "I would want the shuttle bus to be there so I can get quickly to class," Jill says. "I have never missed it when two things are present; when I need it, and I'm not frenetic about getting it. At the end of the day when I am returning to the parking lot, I sometimes have to wait. But, then again, I usually can afford to wait at that time, since there is no rush."

———◆◆◆◆———

Paul, a university student, lost his meal ticket while skiing at a popular ski area about one hour's drive from his school. The meal ticket entitled him to a certain number of meals in the university cafeteria. "It will show up," he thought. "I never worried about it.

"It was only three days later, when I was getting hungry and couldn't mooch off any one else, that I figured I'd better report the card as missing, and get photographed to get a new card. I still wasn't concerned, although I began to wonder if I was really meant to get a new card, since the old one hadn't showed up, and I was so sure it would.

"While entering the building where they issued the new cards, I ran into a fellow classmate who had been skiing the same day I lost the card. She said she had been meaning to call me, because a guy she had met at a rugby match at another university (about four hours away), had given her my meal card.

"What happened was that my card was found by a student from another university, who attended the same rugby match my classmate was attending, and recognized her by the university sweatshirt she was wearing. He happened to be carrying my meal card with him, and came over to her and asked her if she knew the owner of the card. If so, would she be willing to return it to him? I can't say I cared a lot about the card, although I had this strong feeling I would get it back. What surprised me is the series of amazing 'coincidental' events that led up to its return."

———————

David was working at a local bookstore and, with his wife, had signed up for a yoga class meeting at 5:30 on a Tuesday afternoon. "My manager hadn't conferred with me, but he had me scheduled to work from 2:00 to 6:00 that day. A schedule change would have been a nightmare. I told my wife I couldn't go because I didn't want to cause trouble and risk losing my job. I "let go" while still seeing myself in the yoga class, and let it be okay if I couldn't attend.. I didn't fight it.

"I reported for work that Tuesday, and at 4:00, the manager asked to see me. 'We're having a slow afternoon,' he said. 'We wondered if it would be okay if you only worked until 5:00 today.' I said I would be glad to, since I had other things to do. This was quite amazing, because she has never asked me to leave early before. She has a real fetish about keeping to a schedule."

———————

Another member, Patty, related two examples where she happened to receive assistance just when she needed it, without much effort, either on her part, or the person rendering the assistance.

In the first case, her son called from a college 200 miles away, saying that he needed his sport coat to attend a semi-formal to which he had been invited. "He let me know that his friend was at home and lived about an hour's drive from me, and that if I could get it to him, he would bring the coat to my son at the university. You can imagine my thrill when I learned I would have to drive to Vergennes to deliver a coat, during an already full holiday weekend! At any rate, I didn't get upset because I figured it would all work out. And, of course it did.

"The next morning when I went grocery shopping, I saw a friend and we chatted about our college freshmen. I happened to mention about my son and his jacket, and she told me that the next day her family was going to the city where I was supposed to take the jacket, and she would be happy to deliver his jacket for me. She even knew the family! So, as it ended up, I didn't need to find two hours during a busy weekend to deliver a jacket, and my son got what he needed.

"Another example that happened last week was very similar in the way it worked out. I left my car to be repaired while I attended a conference downtown. They had no shuttle service in the evening, so it meant a two hour wait until my husband was free, or taking a taxi. A few years ago I would have worried about how I would work this out, and wouldn't even have been comfortable leaving the car without knowing how I would get it back. That morning I just assumed that it would work out, and of course it did! As fate would have it, I saw a friend early that morning at the same conference, and she offered to give me a ride to the garage on her way back to her home. It wasn't even out of her way."

———◆•••◆———

It is interesting how effortlessly things can flow in day to day living if one "allows" them to. Letting go and trusting in the outcome is very important in manifesting. It is not even necessary to inconvenience others, although they can be important facilitators of personal needs.

In the next case, it appears that a person can effect the functioning of machinery. Bill works for a large computer manufacturing company. "My job is to maintain our customers' computers. The limit of my territory is about a three-hour drive from my house. If a problem should happen, I need to be available with a quick response time. One of the benefits of my job is I have some free time if my customers don't need my services.

"I am also remodeling my house, so, if my customers don't need my services, I can work on my home. Usually, I have a project I am working on, and I will visualize the finished product, and the steps to get to the finished project.

"For example, if I am working on the landscaping, I visualize how the whole house will look with the landscaping already done. I start with a clear picture of the finished product. Then I visualize the incremental steps. I visualize what it will look like when I get the first section excavated. Then I visualize what it is going to look like when I pour the first slab for my stairs, and what it is going to look like when I pour the second slab. Then I decide how long it is going to take. Each step I see clearly. On the days that I visualize this, my customers' machines work just fine. I have very few customer problems. When I do, they are on the days that I don't have a project planned.

"Now, a fellow worker in an adjacent territory is always busy. He doesn't have any more more machines or customers to support than I do, and the complexity of the equipment is about the same. But, he always has a couple of calls a day. He never has any free time. This person strikes me as someone who has a negative attitude. He is always arguing with the home office about how they did something wrong that is causing all these problems in his area. He seems invested in having them wrong. Anyway the difference between our workload is amazing."

———•◦◦◦•———

Are we finding that our thoughts can effect mechanical objects so that they function more or less efficiently? Gayle is a recent college graduate who seemed to be able to fix two machines that were not working. Her dad's snowblower had broken down. He had no money to fix it, and borrowed the neighbor's snowblower, which also broke down. "I felt really sorry for him, and went up to my room and concentrated by visualizing the snowblower working. I wasn't sure how it would be fixed but I visualized it working, and turning, and blowing snow. I told my dad to try it once again before he brought it back to the store. I don't know how it happened, but he turned it on, and it was fixed."

Gayle also told us about a generator with a corroded sparkplug at a summer camp. "My husband said he couldn't get it started. I told him to relax and went into the bedroom and meditated on the generator. I had only heard it work once, but I meditated on it sounding the way I remembered it. I told him to try it again. He didn't even attach the spark plug wire, which is necessary to start it. It ran fine the whole time we were there. He called my dad, and told him it was a miracle. Although I was happy that it worked, it didn't seem that much of a miracle to me."

———•◦◦◦•———

Later we asked Sir Garrod about Gayle's repair manifestations and he replied simply, "There really are no limits to what you can manifest, save those you impose on yourself.

Your female friend did not know much about machines, which probably helped her fix it with her consciousness. Had she believed in the illusion of the solidity of the object, it would have been much more difficult. After all, a machine can't run without a sparkplug wire, or so you believe."For most of us who know something about machinery, our beliefs are too strong to manifest an engine running without a sparkplug wire. On the other hand, there is no reason not to believe this woman, who is very honest and intelligent. The difference is, she doesn't have the same belief about the impossibility of a generator running without a sparkplug wire.

The ultimate stuff of the universe is energy, Sir Garrod reminded us. Physical reality is essentially non-substantial. "Your friend sent out energy to the object, the machine, which is just energy, remember. What seems like an object to you, is just energy vibrating at a slower rate. Her energy affected the energy of the object, and transformed a portion of that energy. She expanded the energy. That is, the atoms in the object were spread out, so they were less dense and vibrated at a faster rate, and therefore were temporarily flexible. Then, when the desired result was accomplished, her energy was withdrawn back into her aura. It never really left her. It simply extended out from her, and then withdrew back into her.

"The process of visualization showed the machine what to do. And, the machine has a natural tendency to align itself properly according to its function, in the same way that a sharp blade tends to resharpen itself after use. Now, ultimately you are not connecting with the energy of the machine, per se. You are connecting with the energy of all that is. And since you are part of that energy, there is no separation. It is quite natural for the energy to align itself for its divine purpose."

This concept is a tremendous stretch for our belief systems. To us, objects are solid, not flexible energy waves influenced by the nature of our thoughts. Certainly, as pointed out in *Manifesting Your Heart's Desire*, affecting mechanical objects was one of the most challenging manifestations for most of us. For the manifestor who fixed her car engine with her thoughts, much to the amazement of her mechanic, this was not such a big stretch in her beliefs. She knew nothing about car engines.

This does not mean that manifesting easily in one area is automatically associated with effortless manifesting in other areas. The same person who found it relatively easy to fix her car engine had a great deal of difficulty manifesting a romantic relationship.

Perhaps the most unusual example of the web of interconnectedness had to do with a group member who had to communicate with a wild animal in order to save its life. It is common knowledge that people often have a strong bonding with their pets and feel they are understood by them. We also knew the book *The Secret Life of Plants* by Tompkins and Bird, in which they report experiments showing that man and plant share a cosmic energy which enables them to communicate with each other. Citing some amazing experiments, the authors describe how plants can pick up human thoughts, react to human emotions, and even respond to thought directions, such as opening a garage door.

In the case we recount, the focus is not on the plants themselves, but on the animal intent on destroying those plants, and the good Samaritan who wishes to save the trespassing animal from execution.

Susan had always wanted a garden, but had either been too busy to nurture one, or lived in an apartment where there was no plot of land available for growing. "Well, I talked my mom into doing a garden with me. I thought it would be a good project for us to work on together. I also wanted to experiment with the methods used at Findhorn, based on the books I had been reading. I planted food especially for the animals. I tried to let them know about my plans. I talked with the plants, and truly loved what I was doing. The garden was really doing great, and my mom was tolerating all this 'crazy' stuff. She even liked having crystals in the garden, and somehow accepted they were helping the cause.

"Then it happened! Plants were being eaten at a furious rate. The plants were just beginning to show a lot of foliage. A woodchuck was eating our plants. I talked to him daily, every night after work. I would inspect any damage, and plead with him to leave. But, he wasn't keeping with the deal that I had set up.

"Well, mom, who was not confident about interspecies communication, was not so tolerant. She began to express more aggressive ways we should be dealing with him. For about a week, I successfully held her back from commissioning our neighbor to shoot the woodchuck.

"Finally, one night I came home, and my mother was furious. The little punk had not only feasted on the string beans, but then proceeded to sun himself in the middle of the garden. She ran him off, and informed me that she was taking things into her own hands.

"Upon hearing this, I went into the garden and let the little guy have it. I told him this was it. I'd reached the end of negotiations. If he showed his face again, he's dead. I tried to stop it, but at this point I was washing my hands of him. In no uncertain terms, I told him that if he wanted to stay alive, he had better not come back, because there was nothing I could do to save him.

"For three nights, my neighbor sat on our back porch with shot gun in hand, waiting for that woodchuck. The woodchuck never returned. Months later I asked a channeled entity about the woodchuck. He told me not only had I gotten the message to this one aggressive woodchuck, but I had also gotten the message out to all his friends and family. We had not been bothered again by any of them, though they lived close by."

Discussion

These examples suggest a form of interconnectedness between all of us, including other animals and inanimate objects. They also teach us how important it is to trust the unfolding process, because we rarely have the foresight to predict how the desired goal will be attained.

Paul, Jill, and Annie were able to attract the right people to them to provide the help they needed. In Annie's case, her friends were able to respond to her needs for entertainment just when she needed them.

Patty was able to meet people who made connections for her that eased her own obligations. Moreover, these helpers were not only willing to assist, but their effort on her behalf was minimal, since they were already going where she needed to. How did they know of her needs? She hadn't talked with them. Somehow, there was a level of communication going on outside of their awareness.

It seemed more than coincidence that Paul ran into the classmate who had met the person who found his meal ticket. She was visiting the university where the student who found the ticket lived, they both attended the same athletic event, he was carrying the meal ticket with him, and he recognized her because she was wearing a sweatshirt with the logo of the university that issued the meal ticket.

Were the woodchucks telepathically picking up Susan's warnings? It certainly seemed that way to Susan. So often, with pets and plants, we feel we have an empathic bond, and a way we can communicate with them.

Is there also communication with inanimate objects on some level? Can computers respond to the thoughts, beliefs, and needs of humans? Even with evidence for thought/machine interconnectedness, our beliefs make it difficult to accept this possibility.

Does everything have an energy that is connected with all other energies on a level beneath our consciousness? Are all energies able to communicate with each other on that level in ways that create a harmonious flow of events with our day-to-day experiences in the physical dimension of existence?

Of greatest interest to us is, how we can learn to activate this process on a more moment-to-moment basis? Is it possible to live our lives relatively effortlessly, manifesting all our desires and attracting appropriate support whenever we need it?

Patty, who was so able to attract assistance when her son needed his jacket, or when she needed transportation to where her car was being repaired, had a great deal of difficulty manifesting a satisfying job. In one job situation she reported that she "felt out of control as if I wasn't living my own life. I found myself feeling and getting ill a lot. I was often filled with fear, and frequently found myself hoping for some intervention so I could get out of the job."

Consistent manifesting is not usually learned overnight. Often, there are less-conscious beliefs about ourselves and others that can interfere with the desired outcome. We need to recognize those unconscious beliefs and how they manifest. We may try to manifest abundance in our life but be unable to do so, because below the surface of our consciousness we have a belief that we are not deserving of abundance.

Conclusion

The significance of manifestation in the major theme of interconnectedness, is that it helps to explain why we are able to create through thought to the outer world. The alternative explanation is that it is all coincidence. Certainly, there is always the chance that the incidents discussed in this chapter are coincidental, and have nothing to do with a larger spiritual plan influencing everyday life experiences. These examples do not rule out that possibility. The persons involved have little doubt that their experiences were not coincidences.

If we do choose to account for manifestation through a form of interconnected energies, then we are talking about a higher intelligence. Not only do experiences and objects seem to manifest as a result of conscious desire, but the process is often impossible to predict. There must be some intelligence that accounts for the connections that unfold while generating the desired outcome.

Sir Garrod also offered some encouragement when he told us that as we evolve in consciousness, and become aware of our multidimensionality and existence as energy beings, we can become more conscious of our interconnectedness. This, in turn, will lessen the sense of separation and isolation we feel. In this way, the illusion of separateness is transcended.

"You can learn to consciously connect with the souls of minerals, plants, and animals by using your imagination and abilities of higher telepathy. As you become more familiar with your inner world, you will be better able to reach a greater state of unity with all things; all animals, vegetation, and minerals. You will still retain your individuality and sense of self. Being able to see and feel from the perspective of all the many diverse forms of life, will allow for a greater sense of oneness, of compassion, of wisdom, and of love."

McDermott pointed out to us that, from his expanded perspective, there was a wonderful balance and harmony connecting everything. All things were interdependent, and when each was expressing its own unique talents and abilities to the fullest, it was automatically contributing to the creative expression of all other entities.

"If you could but see how everything in your physical dimension is so beautifully balanced, coordinated, and interdependent, you would always want to follow the guidance of your inner spirit. Each entity, from the smallest atom to the largest celestial body, is exploring its own unique potential, yet in perfect harmony with every other entity's exploration of its unique potential. When you are totally aligned with the divine inner guidance which assists each entity to explore its uniqueness, you are in total harmony and support of every other entity with which you are connected. So by exploring your unique part to the fullest, you are also contributing to some larger entity exploring its unique part to the fullest."

Chapter 3

There Is Purpose to Life's Experiences

When we consciously manifest a desired experience or object, we may employ a variety of active techniques, such as affirmations and visualizations. Or, we may simply trust and allow the solution to present itself, as shown in the last chapter. When we were not as successful with our manifestations, we became conscious of how our subconscious beliefs were manifesting in our lives. All of these manifestation experiences implied the presence of an invisible web of connected energy between thoughts and matter.

However, there were many experiences in our lives which could not be attributed to either conscious thought, or unconscious belief. According to McDermott, Sananda, and Sir Garrod, there was another intelligence, soul, or spiritual part of ourselves, affecting us and residing in another dimension outside time, space, and the physical. This part of ourselves was also manifesting experiences in our daily lives. Arising neither from our conscious desires nor our less conscious beliefs, these manifestations of the third kind were often powerful learning vehicles. But, how could we get in touch with this dimension, and observe its presence in our day-to-day physical existence?

If you are a Flatlander living a two dimensional existence, how do you recognize, and then comprehend, what it is like to live a three dimensional existence? We had been told by Sir Garrod that, even though it may be difficult for us to understand the reasons for the presence of some events in our lives, we are constantly creating opportunities for growth and learning for ourselves. A benevolent form of our own intelligence, often beyond our immediate consciousness, provides guidance for us as we travel a flexible life path. If this is true, is there any way we can see evidence of its presence in our lives? How can we test for its existence?

Although we didn't know how to obtain direct evidence, we felt it might be possible to find indirect evidence. If we viewed our experiences in retrospect, would it be possible to discover how our lives unfolded, in a more meaningful way than chance could explain? How many of the choices we made, and experiences we had in our past could be viewed as part of a much larger process? Since we were told we were responsible for everything that happens to us, if we understood how this process worked, perhaps we could learn how to use it to our advantage. Could we learn enough about it to direct our path and take control of our destiny?

If we could find evidence for how this plan operated in our histories, we might gain more control through seeing how immediate circumstances were actually unfolding as part of our own growth process, and even manifesting our conscious desires. If we could understand more about the technique this less conscious part of ourselves used to guide our daily lives, we believed we would experience less anxiety, grief, and our lives would progress more smoothly.

When we, the co-authors of this book, first met, we felt we had known each other before. We wanted to know why we were immediately comfortable in each other's presence.

As we looked back over our own lives, it seemed to be much more than coincidence that we ended up meeting each other.

Fred's Story

When my wife was offered a position at the University of Vermont in Burlington, Vermont, I thought my dream to return to New England was fulfilled. However, at that time, there was no opening for me in the university's sociology department. There was, however, a position at Middlebury College, thirty five miles south of Burlington, which was very appealing at the time. One of my specialized areas of teaching is in the sociology of the family, and Middlebury's opening accommodated that interest.

For the first two years, we lived right on the campus of Middlebury college and my wife commuted almost daily to Burlington. But, eventually, we both were drawn to living in Burlington, and very effortlessly found a beautiful apartment. A member of my wife's department was moving and told her about the place they were vacating, which was near a park bordering on Lake Champlain. Living near the lake had great appeal for me. We both loved it immediately; it was affordable, and even the fact I would be the one commuting did not seem like a deterrence.

I arranged my courses so I only needed to be at the college four days a week. My manager reluctantly agreed to this proposal. I loved studying in the library at the University of Vermont, visiting their bookstore, and being on campus. I found myself spending far more time using their facilities than those at Middlebury. For some reason I felt more at home at The University of Vermont than I did at Middlebury College. I had difficulty getting to early classes and asked if I could skip the lecture portion of jointly-taught courses where I was not the lecturer. Almost no other faculty member commuted the way I did, and this request was only reluctantly agreed to. Although the ride down to Middlebury was through some beautiful countryside, I rarely enjoyed it, and some winter days were a struggle, when the roads were icy and snow covered.

I could not admit to myself that I no longer enjoyed teaching at Middlebury. I did not feel any connection with the campus or the individuals with whom I worked, beyond a cordial collegial relationship.

Without notifying my department chair, I began making inquiries at the University of Vermont, but a position with my specialities was not available. I also didn't pursue applying for an opening with any conviction, fearing that if my interest was discovered by my chair, my already deteriorating position at Middlebury would worsen. I would be seen as not committed, which was true, but nothing I cared to admit to myself, much less to anyone else.

I didn't know what would happen should I lose the job at Middlebury without having a definite job offer at the University of Vermont. The daily commute, particularly in the winter, became more and more burdensome. I became increasingly frustrated with my situation, but lacked the confidence that I could relinquish my job at Middlebury, and obtain one at UVM.

Eventually the inevitable "tragedy" happened, and I was fired from my job at Middlebury. My self esteem plunged. What would I do without a job? One part of me felt terrible, while another part of me secretly felt relieved. However, I did not dare admit that "secret" part, and went through considerable fear, anxiety, and sadness. Not being conscious of the possibility of a larger, beneficial, pattern, all I saw was the immediate effect. I was jobless, and had no immediate prospects for a new job.

Fortunately, my wife was employed, so we weren't financially desperate. However, she was pregnant with twins and there was some question of whether this was the right time to start a family.

Although I had no job, no full time position was likely to be available in the foreseeable future, and we had twins on the way, we loved our apartment and its location. I still enjoyed doing research while on the university campus. It wasn't a conventional decision, but what made most sense at the time was for me to assume major parental duties when the twins arrived. This arrangement would still allow me to do some professional writing, which I could accomplish at home, and test my theory that men could parent as well as women. My research at that moment was based on the methods women politicians used to balance the demands of public life with private family life. How demanding was parenting, and how were career choices influenced by the decision to be a parent? Funny, I was living what I was researching. My research subject matter and my life experience never seemed as close as it did at that time.

My experience as a father was intense and fascinating. Being fully involved and responsible for two infants' well being was a full time job beyond anything I had ever imagined. It was enjoyable to watch them grow so rapidly in their motor skills, and take such delight in their progress.

I would not have had the same opportunity had I continued to work and commute to Middlebury. Certainly I would not have had the same amount of time. Would I have enjoyed the experience as I much as I did if there were daily class preparations, exams and papers to correct, and a two hour commute each day? Would I come to appreciate how rewarding, and how difficult, it was to patiently nurture and love a helpless infant, or, in this case, two infants? Since my major teaching areas were marriage and the family, the experiences I gained as a parent also provided information I could draw on for the classroom.

While parenting and writing, I made my presence and availability increasingly known around the Sociology Department at the University of Vermont. While I was in graduate school, I developed a specialized interest in the sociology of aging, and the Chairman of UVM's Sociology Department encouraged me to teach a new evening division course on this topic. During the days, I was still available to minister to my infant sons' needs, while having plenty of time to complete my research project, and prepare for and teach a new course. I began checking local community services for the elderly for potential research projects. My experiences as parent and an academician were certainly spanning the life cycle.

My day role as parent and night role as teacher seemed to work out. The new course was popular, and the administration was interested in developing a multidisciplinary specialization in this area. The following year, the chairman asked me to assume a three-quarter's-time position. I loved the teaching assignments and enjoyed the students, which was in contrast to my feelings during my last few years at Middlebury.

Without any promise of a future permanent position, my wife and I bought a new home located less than three blocks from the university. We didn't consider finding two new positions at another university. On some level, I knew I belonged in Burlington, and that things would work out.

The new house came to us very easily. We told our pediatrician we were looking for a new home. We had actually been looking for only a couple of weeks, and briefly toured one other house. The doctor told us of a home that the owner was trying to sell on his own. First, my wife checked it out. She loved its architecture and style. I followed with a visit, and loved the yard for gardening and as a play area for the children, and also loved the large back porch that overlooked the yard. We both loved its downtown location, which was only a five minute walk to the university. In a matter of a few weeks, we were the proud owners of our dream home. It had all the characteristics we both wanted, and was affordable, even with my part-time salary.

The following year, a position in the area of family opened up in the Sociology Department. Because they were a large department, they also valued my other speciality area in gerontology which I had not been able to teach on a regular basis at Middlebury College. In spite of hundreds of applicants, I eventually was selected for the position. Had I applied while at Middlebury College, I would never have been chosen for the position. But, because I was available to teach part time, I had been given a chance to try out before other applicants were even considered. There was little question in my mind that I would have been overlooked, just as I had when I earlier applied, had I been teaching at Middlebury. My desire to teach at the University of Vermont had been realized. My firing from Middlebury College was a blessing in disguise, though I only see that now in retrospect.

Instead of commuting thirty five miles, I now lived three blocks from my job. A daily two hour drive was eliminated. I was involved in challenging and enjoyable community services as a researcher through the local contacts I established in the community. Although I couldn't see it at the time of the hiring, in a couple of years my recognition as a gerontologist would result in a generous national research grant, and a few years after that, a book published by a highly reputable university press. Because of the size and diversity of the department at UVM, my career took off in ways it never could have at Middlebury. The library and other campus facilities where I had always felt at home were now directly supportive of my new position

Also, in the interim, I had an opportunity to parent which I would never have experienced as fully if I had continued teaching full time at Middlebury College. It turned out to be a fascinating parenting experience that I could use for illustrative material in my classes for years to come.

Now, in retrospect, I see how being fired had set off a chain of events that resulted in challenging growth, and professional and personal joy. At the time I didn't clearly see the beautiful patterns unfolding. It is highly unlikely that, even had it happened today, I could have anticipated all the many opportunities that evolved and presented themselves to me. However, had I at least trusted that all events were presented for my highest purpose and learning, then I might have saved myself worry, guilt, and self-recrimination.

All along, was there a part of me providing guidance beyond my consciousness to influence me to seek a new job and locate in this community, so I would become an active researcher and participate with others who were seeking for links with their own higher selves? Did my higher self help me meet the particular person who would not only become a great friend, but my partner in research?

Todd's Story

I was in my mid thirties, living and working in Kingston, New York. I had an excellent job with IBM. I was able to purchase my own house, a nice, ranch-style, three bedroom home in Old Hurley. It was at this point in my life that I met my wife, Sheila. After knowing each other for over a year, we decided to live together. Even though my house provided all the room and comfort we needed, it was still my house and not *our* house. We wanted an older home with lots of charm, on ten acres of land, which would give us privacy. There would need to be a place for our new baby grand piano. We wanted a large kitchen, because Sheila liked to entertain and nurture through food. We also wanted to live within twenty minutes of our work. We contacted a real estate agent, Barbara, who understood the market and listened to our wants. She showed us all the houses that fit our parameters. Not one had the right balance for us. We knew we couldn't find the perfect house, but there seemed to be a major disadvantage with each of these houses. Barbara kept us informed of all properties that we would be interested in.

We were attracted to an old stone house in Old Hurley that had all the charm and room that we wanted. We were getting ready to make an offer, but the owners had to take it off the market because of a law suit.

Another house did fit our requirements perfectly, but the price was way over the appraised value. We liked the house so much we bid over the appraised value, and the owner did drop his price. We got to within $2000 of each other, but neither of us was willing to stretch any further and the deal fell through.

After we went through the emotional loss of not getting that house, we could see more clearly that the house needed more work than we initially thought. It was interesting to note that two months later the owner said he would meet our last offer. But, at that point we were more aware of what the house was really worth. Again, we could not agree on a price.

Both of us were puzzled by the difficulty we were having buying a house. It didn't seem that difficult for any of our friends. We didn't feel our requirements or our resources were all that unusual or that unique. We kept on looking.

In August, a little over a year after we had begun our search, we decided to take a short motorcycle vacation through Vermont. It was a spur of the moment decision. On the third day, while passing through a small town called Essex just outside of Burlington, we noticed a horrendous, large black cloud on the horizon, coming rapidly towards us. I turned to Sheila and asked, "Now what do we do?" Sheila looked quickly around and noticed a real estate office just across the street. "We can go in there and pretend we are house-hunting," she said.

While the storm raged outside, we pretended to be interested in locating a house in the area. The first man, the manager of the office, rolled his eyes in disbelief, but did call over a junior level associate by the name of Mike. I could tell he was eager. I figured Mike probably hadn't had much business lately.

Well, it was still raining outside, so I thought we might as well continue the act. Sheila and I started to list the characteristics we were looking for in a home. I figured I might as well include some detail, since the storm was right overhead. We certainly knew what we wanted, after having spent over a year looking at homes in the Kingston area.

After listening to our description, Mike seemed to reflect for only a moment and then said, "I think I have what you are looking for and it isn't too far from here." With that, we all left the office just as the sun was coming out.

The home itself was exactly what we were looking for. It had all the characteristics that were most important to us. There were only two problems: first, the home was too expensive; and, second, we were not planning to move to Vermont. Nevertheless we ended up giving Mike our name, and told him to notify us of any new developments. Looking back, this struck us as strange. After all, we had no intention of relocating.

Shortly after returning to Kingston I was given an assignment to go to the IBM site located in Essex, Vermont to assess the skills they needed to match up with the skills of the people we had in excess in the Kingston branch. At the time, it occurred to me to reflect on what it would be like to live in the Burlington area. My wife and I had not given this any kind of serious thought on our previous motorcycle trip.

I looked to see if any of their needs matched my own skills. I quickly put it out of my head, because they weren't needing manpower in any of my areas of expertise. But, I kept thinking about it.

When I mentioned to Sheila about the possibility of moving to Vermont, something clicked within us. At some level it felt right. We decided not to take action, but to think about the possibility. After all, it was a big move. We would be leaving all our friends. I had a great job where I was, and there were no jobs for me in Vermont.

Shortly after my visit to Vermont, the Kingston plant announced it was downsizing, and I was given the assignment to reduce the number of people in my department by one. None of the ten people in my department seemed expendable. I needed all of them. Their skills were not interchangeable. In fact, the only one who was expendable was myself.

Somehow, it made sense to consider a move. If I could get a job in Vermont, that would solve the department's needs. I went back to my manager and told him that if I could get a job in Vermont, I could reduce the head count in my department by one, which was my assignment.

My manager said he knew the laboratory director up in Burlington, and that he would give him a call. When he first called, there were no openings. The lab director said that there were no openings now, but he would take a look as a favor to him.

I went up for the actual job interview a week after that. It was on a Tuesday. In the meantime the realtor was writing us about how the price of the house we looked at earlier was coming down. So, when I interviewed, I liked the job opportunities offered me. We felt if the job was offered we would move to Burlington.

While we were in Burlington for the job interviews we looked around at homes, including going back to the place we liked the first time. Even though the price had come down, it still wasn't at the right price. But we put in an offer that was right for us and they came back with a slightly higher price, which we settled on.

So, I had a contract on a house even before I had a job. All this happened in four days. The next day I went to the bank for a mortgage. I didn't know it at the time, but it turned out to be the same bank with which the previous owner had taken out a short term mortgage to build his new house. Because of this previous arrangement the bank was motivated to give me a loan, so the previous owner would have money to pay back his loan. At this time the interest rates were starting to rise. The banks said that if I closed that month, I could be guaranteed that month's low rate which was 10 1/2 percent.

Now, remember that I had just gone for my first job interview. I didn't even know whether I would get the job. I didn't have any guarantee that I would get the job. But it felt right, so I told the bank that I would close in three weeks. I felt that somehow we would make it work.

Rationally, it wasn't a good move, although in hindsight it definitely was, because the interest rate started climbing and didn't stop until close to 18%. Had I waited, I wouldn't have been able to afford the price I had negotiated on.

The closing was held on a Monday afternoon some three weeks later. It was only the previous Friday at three o'clock in the afternoon that I got a call from Burlington offering me the job. They said they hoped I would take it, not knowing I already had purchased a home.

I remember the conversation with the manager. He asked me whether I wanted to come up for a house hunting trip before I started to work. I told him I already had a home. He heard me but it didn't register. Even after I got to Burlington he wondered if I was going to stay in a hotel. He couldn't conceive of anyone buying a house before they even had a job. His belief system filtered it out.

During that three week period, it did occur to me that this was kind of a dumb thing to do. But, I just had a feeling it would work out. I was very confident and never lost any sleep over this purchase and move to Vermont.

From the time we decided to move to Vermont to owning the house was a total of six weeks, compared to looking around in the Kingston area for a year and a half with nothing working out. The contrast was glaring!

We wondered why it had been so difficult to buy a house in Kingston and so easy to find one here in Burlington. While looking for a house in New York, I was putting every bit of effort into it and nothing seemed to work. When I looked in another direction, in this case Vermont, suddenly and effortlessly everything fell into place. It happened so fast. Everything seemed to be so perfectly timed. Everything seemed to just fall into place like "it was meant to be."

Although neither of us had a strong conscious awareness of the process of tuning in to intuition, we were influenced by our hearts. We were drawn to that specific area in Vermont, and even though we were very rational in our views of life, neither of us was closed off from our intuition. Despite living fifteen miles from each other, we were brought together in ways that went far beyond coincidence.

Fred's Story

Just about the time I was finally established with a tenured faculty position at the university, and my twin sons had reached their ninth birthdays, my wife asked me for a divorce. This was a tremendous shock. When my marriage fell apart, the foundation of my life was also badly shaken. Although very happy professionally, I had felt for some time that our marriage was lifeless, though basically congenial.

Following the divorce, I began to look elsewhere to build a new foundation for my life. I began to reach out and explore new interests. One area I had been curious about for some time was psychic research. A special evening program offered an unconventional course in parapsychology.

The class included many exercises to develop trust in the right brain as a source of information and guidance. For someone as left-brained as I am, and in a career that valued the scientific method of sensory-based logic and reasoning, I was greatly challenged, though fascinated as well. We learned a form of meditation that allowed us to view what another person was doing outside the classroom, and to identify the personality characteristics of an unknown person who had worn an item of clothing we held in our hands.

I was astounded at what I was capable of doing. But what proved to be the most intriguing experience was a session in channeling where the class teacher acted as a medium. I didn't know why, but the information I heard from the entity she channeled, who called himself Sir Garrod after a lifetime he spent during the Crusades, seemed so valid. After all, there was no empirical or sensory foundation to support the validity of the information I was receiving.

The information seemed to bypass my logical rational barriers to some deeper level of truth. I felt exhilarated when questioning this entity, and some of the information I received proved very practical and deepened my understanding of some of the unresolved problems in my personal life. He also responded to broader philosophical and metaphysical issues that had always puzzled me about the nature and meaning of life.

His answers led to more questions. I invited friends to share the meetings, and watched how he responded to their questions. I learned more and more about my multidimensional nature, who I was and what my purpose was during this lifetime. Often, I would only be guided to answers and encouraged to develop a connection with my own inner wisdom, or higher self. This higher self was the source of all my incarnations, and much more. But, it was Sir Garrod's loving presence which would help me see a much larger picture about my existence than the limited focused version of myself I had previously assumed was my entire identity.

A friend I met at one of the public meetings recommended another channeled entity by the name of McDermott. I was drawn to meet this entity almost immediately, and it was a wonderful compliment to my work with Sir Garrod. I would go back and forth between each entity, often asking the same or similar questions but getting different perspectives on the same issue. At times, it was unsettling that each entity didn't independently come up with the same answer. After all, I had learned as a scientist to seek out consistency of data as a means of validating information. These spiritual entities had access to information that I didn't have, but they were not omniscient. Each entity, without judgment, could tune into, and valued, the other's perspective, but I was to learn there is no one absolute truth and that each had a valuable perspective to offer me.

During several sessions with these entities, I explored the reason for a persistent pain in my left knee. I kept aggravating it whenever I played tennis. My regular doctor had suggested aspirin and rest, taking care of the symptoms and not the problem, but this didn't satisfy me.

I had been learning from Sir Garrod and McDermott that the body is a reflection of energy patterns, and that disharmony in the physical body could often be traced to some lesson that needed to be addressed. My inner self was trying to communicate this information to me via some disharmony in my physical body. For example a very painful condition called tennis elbow was related to my very competitive style of playing. When I changed my attitude to one of relaxed play, the discomfort in my elbow disappeared. In this case it was a very sore knee which did not seem to respond well to traditional medical treatments.

McDermott suggested that I visit one of several energy workers in the area who might be able to help me with the blockage, which presumably was due to resistance to the flow of feminine energy through the left side of the body. One worker, in particular, a man called Peter, appealed to me. I was suspicious of his work with energy, but he did have an appealing, rational way of explaining his methods to me.

I talked with him several times before I actually allowed him to work on my body. I was absolutely astounded at Peter's ability, not only to heal my sore left knee, but his way of using energy through his hands so easily. I could feel the energy shifting as he worked on unblocking and balancing energy throughout my body. His hands actually never touched me, yet, I could feel the energy emanating from them. The ache in my knee became worse, building to a crescendo. Suddenly, like a dam bursting, the pain diffused and went away.

I was in such disbelief that such a method could heal my left knee that I stomped my foot down against the floor, testing it after he had finished. The pain did return although, only slightly. Peter had pushed my belief system beyond what it could accept, and it would take several more months before the knee completely healed. The delay, however, had nothing to do with his ability to heal but with my ability to accept his method of healing, into my belief system.

Peter could wipe out a headache in a few minutes by manipulating energy through his hands. I could feel my body as an energy being, and for the first time I experienced the relation between the energy part of myself and my physical body. I now knew they were very much interconnected because I had experienced the connection for myself. The concept was not just theory.

While working with this energy worker, I mentioned that I was doing a sabbatical research project on manifestation, and was working with a group of people who had agreed to participate in the study for one year. I explained that the project was an outgrowth of a rapidly growing interest in the relationship between consciousness and matter. I wanted to know whether it was really true that our beliefs and desires, in essence, our thoughts, were behind every object or experience that materialized. Were we really that powerful?

I thought that Peter had a skill to offer our group and I personally wanted to learn how to work with energy. I felt others in our group would be interested, so I asked if he would consider teaching a class for us. He agreed to come to our next manifestation group meeting and give a preview of the class he would teach for us.

This was just our second meeting. There was a very large turnout and several new members turned up. I wanted participants to commit to one year of journaling, so I wasn't going to encourage new members after this meeting. One of the new couples who showed up at my house that evening was Todd and Sheila Varnum.

Todd's Story

I chose to retire early from IBM and take advantage of a variety of retirement incentives offered by the company. I was restless, knowing more what I didn't like doing than what I wanted to do with the rest of my life. Also, I had been feeling there was something else I wanted to do, but I didn't know what it was. My wife, Sheila, had a satisfying job, and although some adjustments had to be made with the loss of my salary, generous benefits would allow us to continue living pretty much the lifestyle we had become accustomed to. But, what was I to do with my new time? I had more leisure. I would do more volunteer work. But, something still was missing.

It was not long before I was directed to my new path. Just after I was playing tennis, I noticed a sizable bump just below my left knee cap. It didn't hurt, but I wanted to make sure it wasn't serious.

I went to my family doctor who sent me to a physical therapist. It became clear to me that they didn't know what to do. It was not something they had seen before.

I decided to ask my intuition for the answer (something I seldom did at that time in my life). When I asked the question, the answer was loud and clear. My intuition said that the problem was not a medical problem, but a spiritual problem. I didn't know where to go to get spiritual help, so I went to my friend, Thom.

Thom, a rolfer in Burlington, is quite spiritual, and had many contacts in this area. He made many suggestions, but one just jumped out as what I needed to do. He suggested that I see a channeled entity by the name of McDermott. I had heard about channeling, but never experienced one.

It was a strange experience. The medium turned over her voice to this entity called McDermott, who communicated information through her. Although quite skeptical, I did feel drawn to have this experience. I had little to lose, and I was getting impatient for my knee to heal.

I learned during that very first session that I had an energy blockage on the left knee and that I had created it as a reminder to open up the energy flow on the left side. McDermott also suggested several people who could help me move energy more freely through the blocked knee. One of the healers suggested was a man named Peter, who worked with energy fields.

I chose Peter because his qualifications seemed excellent for the work that needed to be done, except that he was living somewhere in California, 3000 miles away. I learned that he occasionally came to town and stayed with a friend. It became increasingly clear to me that I should meet this healer but I didn't know how.

Then a strange sensation came over me and I had this clear intention. It was not that I wanted to meet him, but that I was going to meet him. I had no concept of how this would happen. I just knew it was going to happen. I trusted it would happen and let it go.

Three days later, at a class I was attending, I was approached by a woman I had never met before. She began to tell me about an interesting man she had met the night before who had just come to town from California. She added, "I don't know why I am telling you this." I realized at that moment that she might be talking about this person, Peter, I was looking for. I mentioned his name and she affirmed that it was the same person. She wondered how I knew. I told her that I had heard about him and that I had been wanting to connect with him.

She gave me Peter's phone number and I was able to arrange a meeting with him for the following Friday. Later, I was to find out that he was only in town for a few days. The whole process from my voicing the desire for this person to our first meeting took one week. I could feel a powerful energy shaping my life. I didn't know what it was. But I did know it was not coincidence.

I was a little apprehensive about my healing session with Peter. How could a person working with some invisible energy have an effect on my knee? I remember approaching my session with caution and skepticism.

When I arrived, I was told to lie down on a massage table. Peter scanned my energy field by moving his hand about eight inches over my body. Among other things he told me was that I had an energy blockage in my left knee. He said this before I told him why I had come. He said that this needed to be healed to allow the feminine energy to flow, which would enhance my intuition. He then placed one hand on my left ankle and the other hand on the upper part of my left leg to adjust the energy flow. When he did this I could feel the energy in my leg. It was like an electric current moving through that part of my leg. I was amazed. I could see he had no electrical devices attached to his arm or hands. Yet I could feel this energy moving through his hands and into my leg.

I was so amazed with his ability I asked him if he could teach this to someone like me. He said he was going to give a class and was giving an introductory presentation to a group of people in Burlington the following week. He said I could come to his talk, but would have to leave because this group had their own meeting right after his talk. I told Sheila about Peter, and that the class was at the house of someone by the name of Fred.

The group sounded interesting and met on an evening when we could both attend. We attended the first meeting and met Fred, who was directing the study. Fred invited us to become members of the group. Although I didn't enjoy writing manifestations in a diary, I didn't mind recording on tapes and talking with him about my experiences. I felt very drawn to the project. I had just retired and had time available. Perhaps this was at least a partial answer to my restlessness. I also felt like I had known Fred, even though we had never met before.

A spark of mutual interest, complimentary talents, an ease of familiarity and communication, and a growing friendship was to eventually blossom into a full blown partnership in ways I never could have imagined. Later, we would learn from Sir Garrod we had shared many lifetimes together, and during one, in particular, we had been twin brothers who were sheep farmers. It was interesting to learn about this, since I have sheep grazing on my property. Looking back it was very evident this meeting was no accident.

I could feel the circumstances bring us together. We were both having problems with our left knees, which we were told represented blocks in feminine energy that when released, would open our intuition. How did the healer know to mention Fred to me when he did, and why did our participation in the project seem so attractive and interesting? It was very different from anything we had ever done. In fact, I was surprised how ready I was to make a commitment to this project for the year which was required for participation. Something drew us into this project, and we decided we were willing to make a commitment. At a point in our lives when we were reaching out for new directions, new opportunities that felt right were presenting themselves.

Conclusion

Was it because we had shared many previous incarnations together that we felt so immediately compatible? We couldn't be sure. We only knew we felt alive and comfortable in each other's presence. It seemed a bit incredible that we had been sheep herding twin brothers and had shared a life hundreds of years earlier. Presumably, we were brought together in this life as part of a larger plan to collaborate on a research project testing the utility and validity of the manifestation process. What was very evident was that we experienced an amazing synergistic energy and joy when we worked together on these spiritually based projects.

It seemed more than just a chance that we, with such similar interests, should find each other. Born within one month of each other, both of us had experienced injured left knees playing tennis, sought out the same channeler who, in turn, suggested a number of healers. We each chose the same healer and had a similar experience and result. We both wanted him to teach us about energy work. None of this was coincidence!

We marveled at how our higher selves were able to orchestrate this meeting, beginning years earlier when we lived in very different regions of the country. We had met each other when our own individual growth was ready to be catalyzed by the gifts and skills we had developed, and now we were able to share meaningfully with each other. Had we met earlier, we might not have connected so intimately, and with such enthusiasm.

Moreover, we met at a time in our lives when each of us could spend considerable time on the research. Todd had recently retired from I.B.M., had no children, and sufficient income so he could choose what kind of work he would participate in. Fred had established himself in his profession, had obtained tenure, and his children were in high school and only a couple of years away from college.

According to the channeled entities, we had come together in this life "because we facilitated each other's growth." But it was not just for our own personal growth that we decided to meet in this life. According to Sir Garrod, "You have come together to facilitate each other's growth *and* to share your learning with still others, so that the messages of love and expanded consciousness can extend out planet-wide. On a more personal level, this excitement, this lightness of spirit which you share when you are working together, is an excellent example of what happens when your consciousness rises on the scale of perception, because your visions, while not identical, are very very similar. Your spirits go hand in hand down this path."

As we jointly looked back over our lives, it definitely felt as though a force or some form of intelligence was manifesting events for us to experience. It seemed to be basically a benevolent energy, although we were not sure we would always be able to recognize its positive contribution. Perhaps it could have a karmic, or even a punishing, quality to it under some circumstances.

This force seemed to have purpose and direction, and certainly could have represented the expression of our chosen paths. This was not to say that we didn't have the choice to resist what it manifested. Whatever its expression, it seemed clearly different from those experiences we manifested from our conscious or less conscious beliefs.

Calling them manifestations of the third kind seemed appropriate. But was this force really "us," an expanded "higher" part of ourselves? At this point, it seemed plausible to assume this was the case, although there was no way to externally verify this. What we could do was accept this explanation of the presence of a very knowing and wise higher self, and then observe what consequences followed for us in how we experienced and perceived events in our everyday life.

Chapter 4

Becoming Aware of Our Experiences in the Moment

Reexamining events from our past is a useful exercise in learning how we generate "manifestations of the third kind" over our life course. It is possible to recognize the patterns which connect events in ways that were not apparent nor meaningful at the time they were unfolding.

As a human in the focused consciousness of physical form, it was difficult for Fred to see how being fired from a job was actually opening the door to new opportunities, not only for a more satisfying job, but also to experience parenthood—an important personal and professional experience. Todd wasn't aware that the inability to find a home in the Kingston area was an important step to opening up to the possibility of moving to Vermont

If this manifesting force of the third kind is really just another part of ourselves, then can we learn to understand its purpose and process and use it to gain some additional control in our lives? Was it possible to understand the force, and could we learn how to use it to make our lives work better and to more consciously manifest what we want?

We wondered whether we could align more our conscious selves with our expanded or spiritual self without having to wait for months, or years, to pass before we were able to recognize this bigger part of us, as we demonstrated in the previous chapter. So much frustration seemed to occur when our conscious self, with its narrow, focused, perception, seemed to be going one way, and our expanded self, with its recognition of the "big picture," was going another.

Examining our past brought us to the conclusion that nearly all of our experiences were potential learning opportunities designed for our benefit and growth. In some cases the learning and understanding could be recognized almost immediately. In others, it later became evident upon reflection, or after we had discovered a common theme across several of those experiences. We became detectives investigating our own lives. The trick was not to prejudge those experiences, but to retain a neutral curiosity and inquisitiveness about what lessons our expanded consciousness was presenting to us.

According to Sir Garrod, it was possible for our lives to become somewhat easier, even interesting and joyful, if we avoided prejudging those experiences. Otherwise, the lesson could become the consequence of judging an experience, rather than what we were to learn from the experience.

Our daily lives are filled with situations that we often find annoying and inconvenient when we first encounter them. Yet, if we can step back and view these experiences with some detachment and hindsight, an understanding of both the process and the substance of certain lessons is often revealed.

One interesting question we asked ourselves was whether we had any conscious choice in selecting the experiences we brought to ourselves. It certainly seemed that dramatic situations, such as job loss or divorce, caught our attention far more readily than less dramatic incidents. Was it possible to learn all our lessons in less melodramatic ways if we paid more attention to the learning associated with our less dramatic experiences?

A Job For Barbara

Our first account is about a person who struggled to apply the seven spiritual principles in her search for a satisfying job. It took her approximately two years to reach her goal, which provided a wonderful time line to see how her changed perspective was important for her life experiences and her self-esteem. Slowly, over time, she learned to place greater trust in herself and her inner guidance. She progressed from relying on her intellect and external sources for advice, to placing greater reliance on her intuition and feelings for guidance. Interestingly, this growing trust in her inner self was paralleled by a growing love of her entire self and an expanded attention to her own personal needs and objectives.

———◦•••◦———

While the children were growing up I had a variety of jobs, most of which were on a part-time basis to accommodate family schedules and commitments. I also spent a great deal of time doing volunteer work, which I particularly enjoyed when it benefited or supported youth. As our children grew older and neared college age, I felt the need to find some meaningful employment which might even approach working full time.

I made a list of the qualities which I wanted in the "ideal" job. The most important consideration for this job was that I could still be available for the family and that the kids' schedules be minimally impacted. Another facet, which was just another nice idea, but which magnified in importance as my search continued, was that the job be one in which I could facilitate others' growth, especially young people's. The first major job offer that came along seemed, at first, ideal, particularly since it involved working with kids and was near home so I could be available for my children. It was as the executive director of a children's museum and paid quite well. It was full time with some flexibility in terms of hours. However, the greatest demand on my time would be during the summer and during school vacations when my own kids would be home, and that disturbed me.

I agonized over the decision of whether to accept the position. I made numerous lists of the pros and cons of working there. I tried to make it a very rational process and became obsessed with finding the right answer. Throughout the process my stomach churned constantly, and I felt generally unsettled and nervous. When I thought about accepting the job, I felt sick, and when I considered turning it down, a sense of relief would overcome me. My body was trying to give me the answer, but instead of listening, I was trying to justify accepting the job because of its good pay, flexible hours regarding the children, and convenient location.

I even asked for an extension to make my decision. I asked everyone around me for their input...my husband, children, friends...even Fred and Todd! I was trying to arrive at a consensus of everyone's opinion. I sincerely hoped someone would tell me what to do. Ironically, the people I cared about the most kept saying "whatever makes you happy is what you should do." No one would give me a 'yes' or 'no' answer, which frustrated me. I didn't trust my own instincts. I wanted someone else to show me the right path.

Finally, I made the decision to turn down the job offer, but I continued to agonize over that decision even after it was made. I second guessed myself and kept wondering if I had made the right decision. When I added up the pros and cons, the cons outweighed the pros, but I still wasn't sure I'd made the right choice.

A few months later I was offered a job as a career specialist counseling high school students at risk of dropping out of school. It was located in a neighboring town. The job seemed ideal because it met the important criteria of least impact on my family. I would have summers and school vacations off, and I could be home after school with my own children. I would also be helping young people feel more positive about the options in their lives, another goal on my ideal job list. I had been considering returning to school for a Masters Degree in Counseling, and this job offered me a chance to explore that field. However, I had minimal classroom teaching skills, no formal background in career development skills, and no experience helping teenagers find jobs...all qualities needed for this position. Why was I offered this job? Probably because the position felt right for me, and I was able to project confidence in my abilities to the people who were doing the hiring. From the very start, this position felt right...as if it was meant to be.

There is something ironic about the situation in both this job and the previous museum job. Both times, right after I was offered the jobs, my husband had to leave town on business for several days. It occurred to me then, and is much clearer in retrospect, that the universe was giving me an opportunity to realize that I could function quite well on my own, even when big decisions and changes are upon me.

I ended up doing an enormous amount of counseling, some of it very heavy duty, with these at risk high school students. Their problems became my problems and I found myself carrying their troubles into my own family life. I felt smothered since I was using all my caretaking skills on the young people at work, which left me nothing for my family. I felt out of control, as if I wasn't living my own life, but was living in a panicked response to everyone else's' plan for me. I was often filled with fear, and frequently found myself hoping for some intervention so I could get out of the job. Typically, I rarely get sick, but I found myself feeling, and getting, ill a lot. It became increasingly apparent that I would have to leave this job, and that the decision was one I would have to make on my own, not one that would be made for me. Again, I learned I needed to, and could, rely on myself to make choices.

When I announced my decision to leave at the end of the academic year, I was pleasantly surprised and refreshed by how much the students wanted me to stay. I was overwhelmed at what an incredible influence one can have on young people in a short amount of time. I also felt reaffirmed in the growing understanding that I could listen deep within myself for ways to help these youth and hear answers I didn't know I had. Again, I was experiencing confidence in trusting myself and my own abilities. I continue to this day to see the impact I had on their lives.

For a period of time after the above experience, I put my energy into developing my free lance graphic design business. Interestingly, it was work for which I was trained, but which gave me little or no gratification, other than financial. Having done a great deal of volunteering in the field of prevention and wellness, I was intrigued by and applied for a position at a local university doing the graphic design for the wellness program. I was the runner-up for that position, which I took as a reminder that it would not have been in my own best interests to have taken it. Although I loved the program, I would have been doing graphic design as opposed to the people work which I really love.

Several months later (while I was vacationing at Lake George and not at all focused on finding a job), I chanced upon an ad for a part time Career Counseling position at a local college. I was very underqualified for the position, but I was intrigued and something told me to apply for it. After all, I hadn't been qualified for working with at risk high school students either! My application was a last minute submission, complete with my son having to bring a printer and my resume to our vacation site. I even had to utilize overnight express mail to get it there on time, but I felt compelled to follow through in spite of the inconvenience.

It appears I was meant to be that part-time career counselor because, in spite of my inexperience, I was hired for the position over someone else who was far more qualified than I, and who never even was called in for an interview. The job is perfect for me right now. I have my summers free, my hours and days are somewhat flexible so I can be available for my own children and for my volunteer interest, and I am actually helping other people find jobs. I also have time to pursue a Masters Degree. A "wellness" component was added to the position which was not included in the original job description. I see that "addition" as further evidence of the universe providing situations and opportunities from which we can grow and learn if we are open to seeing them.

———

Barbara's narrative is helpful to us as we seek to learn more about the process of trusting our feelings and internal guidance. Initially, she experienced much fear around making a decision by herself about a job offer. In the last incident, she was able to trust her higher self about a job offer for which she wasn't even qualified. She wasn't actively searching for a job when the advertisement appeared in the newspaper she read while on vacation. She "knew" the job was for her. This can be compared with her original situation when she agonized over the job offer of museum director, and relied on everyone else's opinion except her own. She has learned to trust in herself, and not to rely on people or authorities outside of herself for the answers.

Barbara is more relaxed, has less need to control outcomes, and is now more respectful of her own individual needs. She remarked how she used to get very upset if something on her to-do list did not get done. "Now if that happens, I say I know there is a reason why it didn't get done. I am much more willing to express my own needs in a respectful way, and I am given many opportunities to do so with the jobs I am involved in. When my supervisor said she might put someone new in my cramped office, I told her politely that would not be good for me. In the past I would have felt like a victim and not have said anything. She respected my desire. I saw this problem as an opportunity to learn and grow."

Another lesson Barbara learned was to respect her own needs around the job she chose. In the beginning, the major attributes she sought in a job centered almost solely around the extrinsic qualities of flexible hours and money, and very little around the intrinsic satisfaction of the work itself. She had to learn to develop her own boundaries, as the high school job for high risk students showed her. How interesting that she was eventually employed in a position which helped others find jobs for themselves. This seems to confirm a basic principle that we often seem to end up teaching others what we most need to learn ourselves.

Barbara's personal experience was also valuable in helping others: the qualities of compassion, friendliness, and understanding the anxiety that goes into finding a job, has helped her be a better counselor.

In retrospect, she can see how each job prepared her for the next. She mentioned that even her earlier part-time and volunteer employment had helped her network in ways she could never have envisioned today in the requirements of her present job. Learning to trust in emerging opportunities without awareness of the future ramifications and without judgment has always been challenging for her. She says, "I can see how each step was taking me where I wanted to go."

Barbara has always given great attention to the needs of her family, and has found that respecting her own needs actually has helped them as well. For instance, she was able to emotionally support her husband when he left a job he had held for sixteen years and didn't like. "I continue to be amazed at how calm and confident I am in his decision. Financially, it can be a real challenge with his uncertain income, mine being part-time, and one child in college with two to follow. Somehow, my own growth in understanding and trust allowed me to give him the space he needed to make the decision to go off on his own, with my confidence and support behind him. I don't know how my continued growth will impact on his experience of joy and success, but I do know that he is happier now that he left his job, and he doesn't feel the stress of my underlying fear as he did in the past."

Barbara demonstrates the process of learning to tune in and trust the guidance of our higher self, rather than relying solely on the intellect to make a decision. She recalls, "I went from being very intent on figuring out what it was I wanted, expending a great deal of energy manifesting that, and then reevaluating my desires if the end results were not what I really wanted. Through a shift in understanding, and acceptance of the vast support of the universe, I now realize that the keys for me are trusting that the guidance does exist, that it is 'all knowing,' and that if I make myself available to listen and be patient, I will receive guidance and support. I now attempt to live my life in thankfulness, being appreciative of what I now have and continue to receive, as well as being thankful for whatever guidance I do 'hear' when I do 'hear.'

McDermott reinforced this belief in relying and trusting in the heart when it comes to making decisions. "Let us say there is a person who has a dream of a new career, and they dislike the one they have. In their heart they know they are not doing what they are supposed to do. It does not fulfill them or their purpose. But they see before them the car, mortgage, the food, the children, and all sorts of things. And, because of all of these conscious worries, they continue on in their daily drudgery feeling half alive. Their mind, because they are focused on this drudgery, continues to attract more drudgery. So they stay in this consciousness because they are afraid to let it go and allow the next and highest thing in their dream to present itself. If that person could completely, in faith, walk into their place of employment and quit, knowing that what they sought was there for the asking, they would find in a very short period of time that the new had come in, and they were on their way. But, it would take belief in their heart to attract this to themselves. Yet, in fear, they will not take the next step. But, it is through the process of running everything through our minds that we keep drawing back to ourselves those things that don't bring us our greatest joys."

In our next account, Andrew demonstrates the value of flowing with the universe and tuning in to his inner wisdom through a series of incidents around his automobile.

The incidents are more immediate, and perhaps less grandiose when compared with finding a satisfying career. Yet, these smaller incidents can prove to be extremely meaningful if one is alert to the choices involved.

Andrew's Story

It was a beautiful day at Stowe. After a morning of great skiing, I decided to try a different pair of skis I had in my van. While exchanging the skis, I inadvertently slammed the door shut with the keys inside the van. The nearest locksmith was ten miles away from the ski resort, and would charge at least seventy dollars. Also, this whole incident would tie up the rest of the afternoon (assuming the locksmith was available and not out on another call). I began to feel quite frustrated at first, as I thought of the stupidity of my action. How many times had I opened and closed the trunk with the keys in hand? Why did I forget to do it this one time? It was a stupid and thoughtless act. I knew I could have avoided the whole incident had I been more focused and attentive to what I was doing.

Then, a thought drifted through my mind. Every experience presented a choice. Perhaps this was just another opportunity to learn about manifesting. Why not assume that this whole incident would resolve itself for the best? Briefly, I visualized myself with the car door open. Slowly, I began to experience the feeling of trust and assurance that this would all work out for the best. I noticed that my mood began to shift from one of mild anger and frustration at myself, to a feeling of trust in a positive outcome and curiosity as to how it would unfold.

My friend, Jerry, came over to see what was taking me so long. He suggested the locksmith (who charged seventy dollars) as a likely solution. I felt that there were other answers which I could not see at this time, so I said to my friend "let's have lunch first and we will be able to see things clearer."

We went to lunch and did not think about the car at all. Just as we were getting up from lunch Jerry said, "Let's ask Sally at the office. She might know what to do."

Sally, as almost an afterthought, suggested that security sometimes can jimmy a lock but there was only one person who had that capability and he might not be available. She thought this was his day off. While not attaching too strongly to this outcome, it was hard for me to mask my enthusiasm and I encouraged her to try and locate him. When Sally radioed him, we found out that he had just started his shift and he could come right over. If we had tried him before lunch we would not have found him.

This did not guarantee a solution because continuous effort was not resulting in success. Again and again, the security officer tried to jimmy the lock open using a variety of approaches. I continued to be positive that everything ultimately would work out satisfactorily. And, again, I did not exclude the possibility that the locksmith would end up being the answer. I was open to many different outcomes, but clearly preferred a simpler and a more timely solution than that of calling a locksmith.

After about half an hour, the security officer was about to give up and I began to think that the locksmith would have to be the answer. Then, it seemed, the officer got a "flash" and said he would try one more way of releasing the lock. In an instant, the lock popped up. Just when it looked like there was no hope, the door opened.

I felt that this was a good example of manifesting by letting go of the outcome, while still desiring a convenient and basically effortless solution. I had trusted the universe to bring me the solution, feeling that there was an abundance of options and that the most obvious, the distant locksmith, was only the most visible one because of previous knowledge. But, I felt other solutions that were not so apparent were also available, and I opened myself, not only to these other solutions, but to a path or process that would lead me to these other options. I did not panic, or put a great deal of negative energy on the outcome.

At that point, my intuition suggested I have lunch first and then attend to the problem. My intellect rationalized that I would think clearer. What I did not know at the time was that I needed to wait until the security man started work.

———

My car was involved in another fascinating experience at a time when I was trying to buy a good, used, lawn mower. I had made an appointment for four o'clock one afternoon to visit some people who had advertised a lawn mower for sale, and who lived about twelve miles outside of Montpelier in a very rural area. The day had been going along well, since I had other errands to do in Montpelier before my afternoon appointment.

I was getting somewhat tired during the day, however, and had decided to cancel the appointment. Several times, when I tried to call, the line was busy. I found myself saying, "Why is the line always busy?" The answer that kept coming to me from my intuition was that I should go. So, against my better judgment, I went.

While trying to find the dirt road that led to the home where the lawn mower was for sale, my car stalled out. I had overshot the road and it was only with some effort that I got the car to start. At that point I decided to forget the appointment, again. But, while repassing the road, a little voice told me to turn down that road once again toward the home with the lawn mower for sale. The name of the road, incidentally, was "Bliss Pond Road."

Things were not very "blissful" though, as my car stalled again about a quarter of a mile down the road. The oil pressure light was on, and a check of the oil dipstick indicated that I was very low on oil. I was down at least two quarts.

Here I was in the woods, twelve miles outside of Montpelier with no homes in sight, or for that matter, any cars. I had not seen a car for the last six miles. I really didn't have any options, other than to wait for a car to come by. Normally, I would be quite upset, but for some reason I was quite calm and curious this time. I knew there was a reason for this annoying event, even though I could not understand its purpose at that time.

Being in a positive frame of mind, I thought to myself that there would be a car coming around the corner "right now." Certainly no more than five seconds had passed before a car came around that corner and a nice lady asked if I needed some help. I thought it unusual at the time that a lady would stop for a stranger.

She didn't know where to get any oil, but she did know where the people lived who were selling the lawn mower and offered to take me there. I told her I hoped I was not taking her out of her way, and she replied, interestingly enough, that she normally went to her home the other way. But today, perhaps for a change of pace, even though it was a little longer, she had decided to take the road I had stalled out on.

When I did arrive at the home which had the lawn mower for sale, I explained who I was and told her about my recent car problem. She was very apologetic, since she didn't know how she could help. She seemed more concerned about my car problems than I was.

I now found myself saying the most amazing thing! I told her, "Don't worry. The problem is already solved. We just can't see the answer yet. Let me look at the lawn mower, and before I am done we will know the solution."

I was amazed I said this, because I couldn't imagine what the solution was. I also was aware that it was the right thing to say and I had total confidence that the statement was true. This was also amazing. Where did the confidence come from?

As I was looking at the lawn mower in the garage, I heard her say "your solution is here." She was referring to her grandfather, who had just stopped by to visit her. I thought it odd that she knew a solution was at hand, since she had not even spoken to him yet. How did she know he could help?

As it turned out, he was happy to drive me back to Montpelier to get some oil. As we were driving, I began asking myself what this was all about. This couldn't be an accident. It was surreal. The answer that came back to me was that this situation was more for him than for me. So I started to chat with him asking him what had brought him to Vermont.

He said he didn't know what brought him here, but that he was adopted and couldn't find his real parents. It had been on his mind all his life. He was now 84 years old. Ten years ago, he found out that he had come from Boston, but they would not allow him access to his adoption file without a court order from Vermont, which the local judge was unwilling to do. He felt he was at a dead end.

I asked him whether this was important for him to know, and he said that it was. Then, for the second time that day,

I surprised myself by telling him in a very certain voice that he should go back to the Vermont court because there was a new judge who would give the permission he sought. Even though I had no knowledge of this, somehow I knew this to be true.

He then replied that he had heard that the old judge had retired, but he still wasn't convinced he should start the whole process over again. Once again, and with conviction, I told him, "It is important that you do this. You will get the information you need this time."

As he returned me to my car, I was fascinated by the strange string of coincidences that had unfolded. Did I have this car failure just to tell an 84 year old man to try once again to obtain what he had been seeking all his life?

I asked him why he stopped to see his granddaughter. He said that his action was actually quite odd for him. He had been home, and then quite suddenly he felt this urge to go for a drive in the country. While out driving around, he decided to stop in and see his granddaughter, which was a departure from his normal routine.

Later, while reflecting on all these events that had transpired, and with the guidance of Sir Garrod, I learned I was not only there to help the grandfather but also the granddaughter. She tended to worry about whether her needs were being met. Hopefully, my calm and reassuring trust in life would, at the very least, make her curious enough to ask herself what I knew that she didn't know.

As for myself, I was learning about the value of trust and flow in my own life. There seemed to be a larger plan that I could not see. But, I could learn to calm myself in the face of uncertain and uncomfortable circumstances, and tune into a higher wisdom and guidance. I also realized how much I enjoyed helping other people empower themselves. There was a real sense of adventure and mystery about the entire episode. And, as it turned out, I got home only a half hour later than I had planned, without the lawn mower, which almost seemed incidental to the entire unfolding of circumstances.

At times, I still wonder whether the granddaughter is a little more trusting of life because of what happened that day. And, did the 84 year old grandfather ever start up the process again and actually obtain the papers he had sought for so long?

There was still another incident of trusting which involved my car, but, in this case, things didn't evolve so smoothly. This time my ego was clearly in the way and the experience turned out to be an excellent lesson about what happens when you *do not* tune into your higher self wisdom.

My father, brother, and I had never played golf together in Vermont, and I was anxious to show them all the choices we have here. My brother, for example, lived in a place where there were very few choices to play, since almost all courses were associated with expensive private clubs. I wanted him to know how nice it was to play here in Vermont.

The first two places we played at were nice, but I didn't feel either one really showed off what we had to offer. The second place was fairly new. Therefore, there were not many people, so we ended up having a nice time. But, because it was new, there were some unfinished things about it. We had much better to offer for a good time and I was determined to prove this to my relatives.

The next day, my father suggested we go back to the somewhat unfinished course because it was not crowded but I, of course, had other plans to play on some really neat courses. I called four other courses, and every one had some event going on that made getting a tee time unlikely. Finally, I called a fifth course, which was not as fancy as the other four, but would be better than going back to the one we played on the previous day which my father had recommended.

They said they would have openings starting at 9:30 in the morning. So, we started out with plenty of time to get there. On our way we had to cross a set of railroad tracks and, wouldn't you know, just as we got to the intersection, a freight train with 114 cars traveling at five miles per hour was just beginning its transit across the road.

Well, we still had plenty of time to get to the course. However, as we were approaching a major five corner intersection, I noticed an enormous back up of cars. The traffic lights were out and the woman in front of me was too timid to go. She just sat and waited.

Eventually we did get through, but by now I was beginning to ask myself if I was in flow, or was the universe trying to tell me something. But, I ignored any feedback, and continued to push on to my original destination. A few miles down the road, I mistakenly followed a detour that actually put us on the road to the golf course we had played at the day before. I was not to be dissuaded, however, and I turned around and rejoined the road we had left for the mistaken detour.

We were somewhat late when we finally arrived at the golf course I was determined to play on. The parking lot was full, except for a few spaces located in the middle of a huge puddle which almost would have guaranteed we would have gotten muddy and wet when we got out of the car.

I did notice one place way up front, but just as I was

ready to park, I noticed a sign saying "reserved parking." I saw someone running from the starting shack towards me. I assumed he was going to tell me I couldn't park there. I rolled the window down, and was quite surprised at what I then said. Instead of asking whether he could help me find a place, I asked whether we should go someplace else. His response was equally interesting. Instead of saying something like "let me help you find a place," he concurred and said that we should definitely go someplace else.

Either of us could have taken the questions and answers as simply meaning to look for another parking place in the same parking lot. Instead, I interpreted it to mean I had finally gotten the message, that with enough things having gone wrong, I didn't want to play there.

I still hadn't completely gotten the message, though. As I drove out of the parking lot, I wanted to pull over to the side and check a map to find still another course to play on. There was no place to pull over, and even no way to slow down with traffic behind me. Again, I noticed that I was on the road heading directly back to the golf course we had played on the day before, which my father had suggested we return to.

It finally dawned on me that we were to return to this course. Well, it turned out to be a day of magic, one of the most enjoyable golf days ever. All of us had a wonderful time. We each excelled in our game and enjoyed being together.

Of course, I don't know what would have happened had I continued to insist on going somewhere else. But I certainly learned a lesson about letting my ego make decisions for me, rather than respecting the cues my higher self was sending. There is obviously a part of me that is better able to solve problems and provide me with the experiences I really want. What we really wanted to experience as a family was a sense of friendship and mutual enjoyment, rather than to see how many fancy, but probably crowded, golf courses were available in Vermont. I have learned that life flows more evenly and simply if I tune into my intuition, pay better attention to outer cues, and just simply get out of my own way.

Ted's Incidents

The immediate reaction in the following incidents is frustration, confusion, and some anger towards self or another. Realizing that nothing is gained by complaining, blame, or through the use of reason, Ted relents, choosing to be guided by feelings and opening to what is being presented to him.

———————

As I think back over the three incidents that made an impression on me regarding the value of intuitive guidance, I am drawn to tell them in order of occurrence. The earlier incidents, the case of the sold out concert and the canceled airplane flight, in a way prepared me for a car accident which followed about six months later. Because of the experience and practice I had with the earlier incidents, it made it a little easier to be neutral and accepting about the car accident. It helps to have experience in shifting perspectives with smaller episodes first being encountered.

With regard to the first incident, I still remember how disappointed I was last summer when I arrived at the opening concert of the Mozart festival and found all the tickets sold. My mother and wife were in a good mood and after some initial frustration (mostly on my part), we decided to take a drive up a mountain for a view of a beautiful sunset. I blamed myself for not anticipating a sell-out, but then decided to take advantage of a beautiful evening for a ride. Both my passengers were quite accepting and cheerful, and their energy actually influenced my perception around the whole incident.

When we got to the top of the mountain, I noticed a large crowd had parked in the meadow. Asking a parking attendant what was going on, she said that the Vermont Symphony was playing, and after hearing my story about the sold-out concert, told all three of us to go on in without charge. We missed the first selection, but had wonderful front row seats for the rest of the concert. I didn't even know this orchestra was playing that day. Or, did a part of me know it was playing; a part that I was unaware of?

On my vacation to Sarasota, Florida, my plane was canceled. I remember standing in front of the ticket counter feeling perplexed but not panicked, while others around me were getting increasingly frustrated and angry wondering what to do. There was a moment when I did blame the airline for lousy maintenance. But, I was more confused than anything else, asking myself, 'Why is this happening to me?' and thinking it was better to fly late and with a good engine than take a chance.

While I was standing there, the ticket agent asked for my ticket, wrote on it very quickly, told me to follow him at a run, and took me to another counter. At that point another ticket agent told me to be very fast and to follow him, which led onto the plane of an airline other than the one I was scheduled to fly on.   At that point I had no idea what had happened, except that I was on a plane. I was clearly the last one on and within seconds the door had closed and we were taxiing for take off. I looked down at my ticket and stared at the scrawl. I was going to Philadelphia as an intermediate stop instead of Newark, my original lay-over where I was scheduled to change planes for Florida.

With some help from the stewardess, I learned I was to stay on the plane during its half hour layover in Philadelphia. Somehow I had ended up taking a direct flight to Sarasota from Burlington. I didn't know this flight existed. Well, miracle of miracles, I actually ended up arriving almost a full hour earlier than the original scheduled flight. Who was taking care of me? A part of me had opened to what was meant to happen and a little miracle followed. I had no control over the departure of the original flight but I was in complete charge of how I would respond to the incident. I could be bitter, angry, and frustrated, or, in my case, bewildered and curious.

I am sure having had those two experiences made it possible to be more curious and open to the experience of the car accident. The accident particularly didn't make any sense, since it wasn't my fault. The guy plowed into me from behind. But as I was to learn, we are all willing participants in each other's lessons at least on some level of learning.

In any case, as I said, while driving my sons to school a car rear-ended us at a stoplight, damaging our bumper but not resulting in any injury. Fortunately, because of the heavy morning rush hour traffic, the person behind me was not going very fast. He said he was daydreaming and just lost track of the flow of traffic.

Needless to say, I was, at first, very annoyed, even angry. I had not shaved or bathed, and was only lightly dressed. After all, I was just planning to take the kids to school, a ten minute drive, and then return home to prepare for work. This kind of interruption was not in my outline of planned events for the day. I like things to be orderly and usually don't respond well to unplanned events. And, of course, I felt upset because the kids would likely be late to school, not to mention all the events it caused, including collecting insurance and arranging for possible repairs that would surely follow.

While I was standing there by the side of the road, it did cross my mind that all events are self-created and had some lessons for us if we could open to the possibilities. I couldn't imagine why I had created this incident, but I did feel anger and frustration drain away from me even while the other driver was cursing himself for his own stupidity. I began to feel some sympathy for him. He had just had a repair job done on the front end of his car and now it would have to be redone. Evidently, this was not a first time incident.

It must have been less than a minute before a policeman "just happened" to be driving by. He stopped and began taking a statement from the other driver. I asked my kids again whether anyone was hurt and they answered in the negative. I then sat back to wait for the policeman to come and take my statement. A few events flashed through my mind reminding me that I should not prejudge this incident. Getting worked up would not change anything that had happened. However, I was in complete control of my thoughts and how I chose to respond to this incident.

The policeman finished with the other driver and now approached me. He took a statement from me and then told both of us to take it from there. Insurance information was exchanged and each of us drove off, the whole incident taking perhaps fifteen minutes from start to finish. The kids were even on time to school. Calls to insurance companies went relatively smoothly.

Estimates by body shops were relatively uneventful and did not seem to interrupt the general flow of daily events. In fact, while in a garage getting a repair estimate, I noticed one tire was almost flat. The body shop worker suggested it might not be a flat tire, but rather a result of the cold weather and offered to add air to the tire. It was the only time it deflated all winter.

Was it possible that because of the need for an estimate, which in turn was a result of the accident, a potentially dangerous and costly repair was noticed and fixed quickly and effortlessly.

What were the benefits of taking a relaxed attitude to unfolding events, centering oneself, and taking on a role of curious observer? All of the preceding incidents involved what most people would have perceived as annoying experiences. With the case of Barbara's job search, major frustration was experienced from the beginning.

In the shorter incidents, a brief response of anger and frustration was followed by a pause, and an opening to experience whatever was to follow. Each person eventually chose to respond to these incidents with a readiness to listen intuitively and learn something about the meaning of the incident itself. This was also the case with Barbara as she neared the end of her search for employment.

By achieving a level of peace and curiosity in the way they perceived the events, these individuals allowed for a natural evolution to the process, and the solutions unfolded with relative ease.

McDermott said that the ultimate first step of any challenge is *accepting*. He suggested that any challenge before us is to be perceived as divinely created. No matter what it is, a car accident, plane cancellation, or serious illness, the response is always the same. We need only accept the process and then completely accept and embrace the learning it entails. No judgment should ever be placed on an experience. This is not always easy to do, of course, when you are in its midst.

The concepts of winning or losing do not exist on the spiritual plane. McDermott remarked, "From our dimension you are never fighting a battle. Rather, you are simply opening up to divine acceptance of the challenge before you, so that the solution which already exists on another plane comes to you. If you don't attach a certain value to yourself in the circumstance, then the circumstance is free to help you expand and evolve."

None of the previous incidents created a situation where the participant was a victim, although they could always choose to interpret their experience that way. One person had created his "mistake" of locking the keys in the car, and another person had attracted the accident to him for some higher learning purposes. With our limited and focused perspective on life, we cannot possibly see all the ramifications of our experiences. We are simply not capable of seeing the grand design or the intricate beauty of all the experiences and lessons taking place at once. Nor can we see how all the different people involved in our dramas could be drawn together at the right times and in the right places to assist others with their shared and separate lessons. Yet, we can come to appreciate the grand design in a limited way, tune in to the hunches coming from our higher selves, and eventually learn to trust the flow of events that unfold before us.

Without proof and without really knowing, we decided to try and live this philosophy to see how its perspectives affected our lives. We paid more attention to our intuition and tended to follow it—even when it didn't make sense. Without seeing how this could be true, we just said that at a higher level it was perfect. In fact, many times our greatest imagination could not see the truths involved.

———◆•➤•◆———

In the following narrative, Jim gives a clear rendition of the events in his life as he tries out this new perspective. He has been very sensitive to his intuition when dealing with some annoying incidents. Moreover, the richness and exuberance that the storyteller finds in his experiences makes this a valuable way for all of us to learn.

Head Learns From Hood about Heart

Why do things happen the way they do? Sometimes when I look back on a series of events, I can see how perfectly they have unfolded. Yet, in the moment of the experience itself, things don't seem to be happening as planned. There are still other situations, where, even with hindsight, I didn't have a clue as to what was going on.

I do know that there is an energy outside of my consciousness playing a large role in what is manifesting in my life. And, if I can sense the direction of this energy and go with it, not only do things work out, but my life becomes a flowing experience. It is like trusting that this river of energy next to me will flow to places that are beneficial, and I have only to just jump into my "inner tube" and allow the current to take me with it.

This is definitely a trusting process, because many times the river starts out in a direction that is different from where my conscious self wants to go. Also, I can't see past the first bend, and who knows what lies ahead!

I have also experienced the choice of not following this energy flow, and then things seem to be a struggle. I always have free choice. If I choose to ride the horse in the direction it's going, life generally seems to work with ease. If I choose to go against this energy, life can still work, but things tend not to proceed as smoothly. The former will often provide me with things that I didn't even know I wanted.

This larger river of energy or intelligence seems to have a broader perspective of my life than my conscious self does. It "sees" much more than I do. I access it intuitively. The more focused and conscious part of me tends to give me what my intellect wants. I tend to access it through reason and logic.

Sometimes when I de-emphasize my intellect and just let my intuitive side flow with the experience, I am amazed at how everything can work out so easily. Yet, I can end up not having a clue as to why that particular path was ever taken.

For instance, I took my car to be inspected at a local garage. I was told I needed a new muffler in order to pass inspection. I felt the owner was trying to make some extra money, so I told him I would take the car to Pete's Garage. I then told Pete's Garage to inspect the car, and do what was needed to pass inspection. They found the car to be in perfect shape and provided a new sticker for the year.

The following morning I had an important meeting connected with my consulting work. The meeting was 40 miles from my house, approximately a forty-five minute drive. I usually make the trip on the interstate but that particular morning my intuition told me to take the back roads.

At that point my intellect disagreed using what seemed like solid logic. The trip would take 15 minutes longer on the back roads, and the time could be better spent preparing for the meeting. Nevertheless, I chose to follow my intuition and took the back roads.

About 15 minutes into the trip, on a stretch where the speed limit dropped to 35 MPH, the hood of my car unlatched and flew up, blocking the windshield. I couldn't see anything, except for the yellow line out my side window.

Using this as a guide, I slowed. down and pulled over to the side of the road. The damage was minimal. The windshield was intact. The hinges on the hood were sprung, and the hood jammed into the cowling. With a little effort, I was able to pull the hood back down, but it would not close.

At this point I could have chosen to be frustrated and upset as I would have in the past. And, in fact, I was quite angry for a few moments. Old programming does not change instantly. After all, this was an important meeting. It had taken effort to arrange to have all the people working on the project meet at the same time. The project was already behind schedule, and I was feeling guilty that it had taken so long to set up this conference. Trying to reschedule this meeting could easily take another month.

But, I simultaneously recognized that there was probably more to this than met the eye, and I decided to go with the flow. Becoming frustrated and angry would only bring more frustration and anger. Since I knew I was manifesting all the time, becoming frustrated would only attract similar energy back to me, and probably create more frustrating circumstances.

Going with the flow meant trusting and being positive. So, instead of choosing anger and frustration, I became thankful that I was not driving 65 miles per hour on the interstate in traffic when the hood flew up. The effect of the hood blowing up when traveling at high speed could have been much worse. It certainly would have been more dramatic. I was also thankful I was on a slower speed limit section of road with no other cars around. Perhaps this was why I intuitively felt I should take the slower back roads.

I chose to return home where I could regroup. My wife decided to make her real estate calls from home before she went to the office and since she didn't have any outside appointments, I could use her car if I dropped her off at her office. I called my client. She told me the meeting had been delayed 2 hours because two key people could not make the earlier time. That was just the time I needed to take my wife to work and drive to my client's office.

It was fascinating to watch the process unfold around this incident. I wanted to stay in the flow. The first two turns on this river seemed real smooth, so I stayed in my inner tube and started to enjoy the ride.

My meeting lasted longer than expected so I called my wife, who was also running late. We decided to have dinner in town after I picked her up. A new Vietnamese restaurant had recently opened that we wanted to try. The dinner there was just what we needed, even though we would not have chosen it with all the things we wanted to get done.

An interesting side experience developed because our Vietnamese waitress could not speak English very well. She got our orders confused with the table next to us. After an interesting interchange using simple English and sign language, we not only got our correct order but the management did not charge us for the entree. Somehow this river knows where it is going and it becomes easier to follow when you allow it to carry you.

That was on Friday, and I still didn't have a car for the weekend. But at this point, I was learning I didn't need to worry. I went to bed not knowing the answer, but trusting that the flow of the river would provide whatever information I needed.

As I was waking in the morning, a solution came to me. The hinge which goes from the hood to under the cowling at the bottom of the windshield is shaped like a bent arm— like the position a person would hold their arm with a closed fist to show a sign of power.

The hinge was bent further than normal, and the hood wouldn't close. So, if I took the hinge off the hinge points under the front of the car, it would allow the hood to close and latch in the front. Also, the hinge would still be under the cowling which kept the back of the hood from moving. It only took half an hour and worked better than I had expected. I now had a car to drive. In fact, it was hard to tell that there was a problem except that when you opened the hood, the whole hood came off the car.

I still didn't know why this had happened. I suspected that the mechanic at Pete's Garage didn't close the hood all the way. The main latch didn't catch, but the safety latch did—at least for a while. But why would the mechanic open the hood during an inspection? Even if he did, how could I prove that he was the cause? I decided not to waste my time—just bite the bullet and get it fixed.

On Monday, I went to my car dealer, who gave me an estimate of $438. But instead of setting up an appointment, I found myself saying, "I will get back to you." Why didn't I make an appointment? The estimate was lower than I expected, and I had no other plans. Even with this thought, I got into my car and headed for home. On my way home, my intuition told me to stop by Pete's Garage.

At this point my intellect entered into the picture. How quick my intellect was to judge the thought. I had no proof that the mechanic had left the hood unlatched. In fact I couldn't even imagine why he would have opened the hood. But I was also going right by there. So, "What the hell!" It would only take ten minutes at the most.

The manager at Pete's Garage was very nice and explained to me that they didn't need to open my hood to do an inspection. When I explained what had happened, he said he would ask the mechanic who worked on the car. After reviewing his records, he called in Joe.

When asked if he had opened the hood, Joe said "no" and then paused and said, "well, just for a short time to check something. He then was asked if he had closed the hood securely. Joe said that he just lets the hood drop, that it worked every time.

The manager looked at me and said that if I gave them an estimate, their insurance would pay for the damage. I told him that I had one estimate with me. At the same time I was thinking, "can life work this easily?"

In a few days Pete's Garage called. They needed a second estimate. The second estimate came in at $686. I explained to Pete's Garage in my fax that the new estimate was higher because the repair shop noticed some damage which the first had missed, and their rates were higher. Pete's Garage did not get back to me. I know what I would have been thinking if this had happened to me five years ago. I would have concluded that they would give me an apology and a run-around, but ultimately nothing would have been done. I would have become very impatient and tried to take control and force the action. The energy behind this desire to make something happen would have come from fear and suspicion—that these mechanics were covering their butts and were not to be trusted. Undoubtedly such energy would have drawn some confirmatory evidence of my suspicions—think the worst and get the worst.

However, at this point in my life I was more in trust. I stayed on the river in my tube by being positive. I called Pete's Garage. The manager said he didn't get the fax. If I would send the fax again, he would get back to me in two hours, which he did. He suggested that I go with the second estimate, even though it was the higher price. He told me to make an appointment and he would have his insurance pick up the bill.

When I made the appointment, they said that they needed the car for three days. The thought that I can't be without a car for that long raced through my mind. I then realized that I was no longer in trust. I had stepped out of my tube onto the banks. I had turned away from the direction the river was going to take matters into my own hands. With that realization, I decided to get back into my tube and see where this is going. After all, I could always get off the river and rent a car, which seemed like a very boring option at this point.

Two weeks later, the car was due at the garage for the repair work. I was aware that things had already begun to fall into place. As it turned out, my wife's schedule and my schedule had us in the same area at the same time, at least for the first two days of the car repair. We could share her car. We did not consciously try to do this, it just happened. This also gave us a block of free time together and lunch— a treat, since we always had a hard time keeping our schedules intact to spend time together.

On the first day, the repair shop was right on our way. The manager said that he had a cancellation and could finish my car in two days. How does the river know all this? I certainly didn't have this type of perspective in any kind of conscious sense. We could pick up the car at 4:30 p.m. the next day.

The second day's schedule had us finishing our own business and going by the repair shop at 5:00. Not only was my car ready, but the bill was already paid. They even fixed an extra item that was not part of the accident at no charge.

As I look back on this experience, it still amazes me how easy life can be when we are in a state of trust. What a wonderful perspective to have on life.

———•◦•◦•———

We were impressed with how well Jim followed his intuition and his ability to flow with the experience as it unfolded. We asked Jim to give us some insight on his approach.

"It is so easy to feel anxious, angry, and frustrated when things don't seem to be going as planned. It is difficult to trust an inner, larger, part of me that sees a much broader picture of what is happening. This doesn't mean that you are totally passive existing in some constant state of 'being.' It is a combination of both 'doing' and 'being.' I still had to <u>act</u> on my intuitive guidance. I had to stop at the Pete's Garage station to receive their evaluation of how the hood might not have latched when dropped. However, the action was consistent with my inner intuition, and thus in tune with the river of energy of spiritual guidance.

"How do I know when I am following my intuition and not fear stemming from my ego? Generally, my intellect follows a very logical progression of association. When I experience my intuition, it seems to come in from the side. When my mind is running things, each thought reminds me of the next thought. My intuition just seems to drop in my lap and has no connection with the previous thought.

"When I can recognize the intuitive thought, I sometimes find myself coming up with rational support after the fact. It is like my intuition makes the decision and then I look around for confirming reasons for why I want to make that particular choice over any other choice. Once again my mind is battling to control the outcome even if it hasn't had a hand in the original decision. It will take what it can get.

"In the past, I greatly valued the intellect and would have done whatever it told me to. I would have chosen to travel on the thruway and to ignore stopping at the Pete's Garage shop. Now, I value the intellect somewhat less. I presently seek a better balance between my head and my heart. I allow the intellect to prepare its case, or to provide reasons after the choice is made, but I always try to make decisions based on my intuition. The intellect is still important but its role is to administer the decisions of the heart.

"This doesn't mean that I am always calm when an incident does not follow what I have planned, or that I can always separate out the thoughts of the mind from the feelings of the heart. However, over time, and with more and more similar experiences, it is becoming easier.

"When I started writing this case report, I didn't know how the hood of my car blowing up into my windshield was useful to me. Yet, the writing itself has helped to clarify the significance of this incident for me. Now I think I understand."

Conclusion

Our initial interest was in learning how to utilize this new superconscious force that we were told was actually a part of who we were. We felt we might be able to control the force through understanding its process. As we looked at our experiences, as well as those of others, we began to realize there were limits to what we could understand. Our consciousness simply could not encompass all the reasons and purposes for our experiences. We were not even capable of determining how to best realize our personal desires, or what intermediate steps might be necessary as preparation. How could Barbara possibly have anticipated the path of experiences that led her to her desired job?

The way to align our conscious self with our larger spiritual self is to learn how to listen to our intuition, and place less reliance on our intellect as decision maker. Intuition, as Jim stated, "comes in from the side."

Sir Garrod made suggestions of methods to use to access inner wisdom, "If you wish to become more conscious of your inner mind, we would encourage you to get into the habit of taking a very little pause prior to taking action or to speaking, to allow time to confer with your inner mind or inner voice. Then, when you have listened for the answer, you can turn the decision for implementation over to your ego,(which is its rightful role).

"Inner guidance usually comes when you are in a quiet reflective state. When you get an urge, don't analyze it. If an urge feels joyful or delightful to follow, it probably comes from your inner guidance. If you come from the heart you won't be seeking, but living in the flow, and what you desire will arrive when it belongs and it will not be an obsession. You have to discover whether you are obsessing about something, or whether you are really in the flow rather than coming from fear. You can be sensitive enough within to know where the feeling originates.

"Your joyful urges come from that part of yourself which has a much broader picture than your mind can conceive of to get what you want. It leads you in directions your mind cannot anticipate."

When we don't listen to that voice, we may end up facing frustration, as Andrew did when he wanted to show his relatives a good time playing golf. That is how we know we are off our path and not following our inner voice. Of course, this doesn't mean we can't force an outcome. But, it usually requires more effort and may end up disappointing us.

According to Sir Garrod, when we hear "what if, what if, what if," we are listening to fear and the ego talking. The ego does not trust anything other than what it knows. It is linked with the intellect, and is subject to what external authorities will approve of. Sometimes it takes patience to reach that inner voice over the chattering of the ego and the intellect. Although meditation may help when first learning to recognize the inner voice, with practice one can learn to tune in almost moment to moment.

Sir Garrod pointed out to us that it is often easier to stay with what we know and remain in the familiar, even though it is very painful, because that first step into the unknown is very frightening. In the last chapter, it was too risky for Fred to give up his job at one college and pursue a more desirable job at another college without some guarantee of success. Sometimes we need a kick start to make a change.

Sananda reminded us to "trust that your higher self will assist you in making your decisions and going in the proper direction. Be assured that the path will always be beneath your feet. However, this does not mean a root won't grow across your path and you will trip a little. But you will still be able to stay on the path. You need to trust in yourself and you need to make that first step forward. Believe me that staying where you are can often be much more painful."

In many of the case histories we studied, the theme of trusting a higher power was central to both the lesson and the joyful learning that accompanied the effortless energy flow. This was true for short term incidents, like car trouble, or longer-term job-related desires.

In the very first case discussed in this chapter, it was frightening for Barbara to trust her own wisdom. She had to learn to let go of control and to be open to the wisdom of her higher self. According to Sir Garrod, instead of trying to control how things turn out "visualize what it is you want, and then let the universe get you there. It is not easy for most humans to do this. By relying on the universe to provide for you, this might not come in the form of the specific type of job you thought it would. It might come in a very different way than you had expected." Barbara learned that process well through her own personal experiences and, when the newspaper advertisement crossed her path while on vacation, she was ready to believe in herself, listen to her guidance, take action, and get the job she had really wanted all along.

Barbara's case can be contrasted with the last study where Jim was able, almost from the beginning, to tune into his inner wisdom and follow its guidance. He allowed a little life adventure to unfold without judgment. Not only did he spare himself much emotional turmoil, but he was able to effortlessly receive some very pleasant surprises in the bargain.

We learned that rather than trying to control or direct this force emanating from our higher selves, it was more advantageous to align with it through our intuitive capabilities. Through practice, we could develop this "listening" skill. The outcome tended to be a more interesting and peaceful life, where our experiences could be viewed positively, and contained lessons which we could at least partially understand. Life also tended, as a rule, to flow more effortlessly, and with less drama. This is not to say that choosing a dramatic life is bad in itself. But we were becoming aware we had choices in how we wanted to learn our lessons.

Chapter 5

Illness

Learning to be in the flow and not judging the process as it unfolds was the major theme of the last chapter. Most of the examples discussed dealt with everyday events which were annoying, frustrating, but not terribly traumatic. You may observe, "So what if the person had a bad day of golf with his relatives. Even if he had to pay to get the hood of his car fixed, it was affordable." What happens when the outcome is of great importance to an individual, such as a problematic romantic relationship, or when dealing with a life-threatening illness? Then is it so easy to trust the universe to manifest what is highest and best? How can we accept having a major disease? How do we accept the process? We ask, "What did I do to deserve this? Why now? Why me?"

It is difficult not to judge illness or disability negatively. At the very least, it causes us some discomfort, some dis-ease. Sometimes it can evoke feelings of great fear and involve major suffering. If our identity, our sense of mortality, is synonymous with the healthiness of our physical body, we can expect to experience fears of threat and helplessness when we become ill. Plans to be carried out, and goals to be reached and surpassed must be modified or abandoned to follow the dictates of the body.

Learning to heal is the theme for John, Tom, and Betty in the following accounts. In some cases they must deal with authority figures and diagnoses that seem to contradict the paths of learning to which they are drawn. There are times they will be challenged to trust their own internal guidance, even when it conflicts with the scientific persuasiveness of modern medicine, as well as the authoritative expertise of the medical doctor. Each learned a great deal, not only about their powers to self-heal, but they also received insight about how they attracted discomfort. They will be challenged to allow a process of healing as much as they might feel compelled to do something to heal themselves.

John's Story

About seven years ago I had a severe case of pneumonia which so weakened me it took me close to six months to be myself again. I was undergoing a lot of stress on my job at the time. The doctors had told me that if you get pneumonia once you are more likely to get it again. This so heightened my fears about getting any kind of chest cold or bronchitis condition because it could easily lead into pneumonia again. I definitely did not want to get another case of pneumonia followed by a long period of recovery.

However, I did get a cold and bronchitis the following winter. To ward off any future development of the condition into something more serious, I immediately began to baby myself. I stopped all physical activity and drank lots of water. I worked very hard on manifesting the elimination of this disease. Most important, I took doctor-prescribed penicillin, which did tend to control and even seemed to cure the condition.

That was until I found out from my doctor that penicillin could do nothing for a virus. As soon as I learned that piece of information, my recovery period from a typical bout with bronchitis went from three weeks to six weeks. Nevertheless, I didn't stop taking the medicine. For a long time I was very careful whenever I showed signs of a cold or bronchitis to take measures to lessen the likelihood of it turning into pneumonia.

I kept this up for several years, until one day while driving to work with a good friend of mine, I noticed he was doing a lot of coughing. I asked him what he was doing about it. He said he would get something from his doctor and that it would be gone in two days. Two days later his cold *was* gone.

It struck me that his cold was just as bad as any I had gotten. Yet, he didn't baby himself. He didn't slow down or take any special precautions. He was as active as ever. But how could he be so sure he would be over it in two days? No medicine could help him with a virus any more than it could have helped me.

It was at that point that I recognized that he had a belief system that was working for him. And, his example really awakened me to the power of the mind to heal. When the doctor told me penicillin didn't help my bronchitis, it eliminated the placebo effect from my consciousness. I also realized I was still coming from a place of fear. I was viewing the situation negatively. I realized that I had to accept having the cold as okay. However, taking the energy away from the condition did not mean no longer desiring to be healthy. But I stopped resisting the illness and felt it was okay if I was not healthy. I *allowed* the healing process to unfold without trying to control it. I realized I had been very attached to getting rid of the condition. There was too much fear around getting pneumonia.

Slowly, I began to perceive this condition differently. Since I had no model to follow, I made it up as I went along. So, each time I coughed I saw it as a positive experience, as my body getting rid of this disease. It was a way to thank my body. With each cough, I thanked my body for expelling the energy which predisposed me to the bronchitis or pneumonia. My bronchitis was there to manifest healing and health.

Over the next year I got bronchitis four times and each time I allowed it to heal more quickly. The first time I got it, it took six weeks before I felt fully recovered. The second time it was over in four weeks. The third time it took three weeks. And the last time I got it, it took only one week to run its course and it hasn't returned in two years.

This was a great opportunity to take what appeared to be a negative situation and turn it into a valuable learning experience around belief systems, attachment to outcome, and the power of the mind to heal the body.

―――――――

Tom has learned to live with chronic asthma for most of his life. He relies on an inhaled medication taken several times daily to control the constricted breathing experienced by his lungs during an attack. Certain conditions, such as cold weather, pollen, freshly cut grass, and dust, can aggravate the condition. Almost any kind of stressful situation can also set off an attack.

Tom was content to accept this process for many years until his medication failed him one day and he wound up in the emergency room while suffering a major attack. This event triggered a strong desire to cure a long-term condition which his doctors insisted was incurable. This intent to "cure" himself brought up a host of issues to be confronted, transcended, and healed; a process still going on for Tom today.

Tom's Story

Every breath presented a struggle, a challenge; gasping, to bring enough air into my lungs. If I didn't get relief soon, I was sure I would suffocate. I had never been so frightened. It seemed my whole body was focused on just one task; to obtain sufficient oxygen so I could relax...so I could finally rest. It was after 2 A.M. and I was exhausted.

I had checked out of the emergency room a scant two hours earlier with the hope the asthma had been brought under control. Now, with a great feeling of sadness, and a sense of defeat, I had to return to the emergency room.

This time the person who treated me earlier was not about to let me go back home. I was told, "Do you know that more and more people are dying of asthma? They wait too long to have it treated. We strongly recommend you check yourself into the hospital and stay overnight."

I knew I couldn't go back home and return a third time. I hadn't had an attack this bad since I was a kid. Maybe my life really was in danger. "I don't understand why I created this for myself," I blurted out between laborious breaths of air.

I felt guilty the moment after I said it, but it was too late. No one could understand what I was saying, and I was in no condition to engage in a metaphysical discussion. I was still too uncomfortable. "You aren't responsible for your condition," said a very authoritative intern. Another said, "You did the right thing by coming to us. Asthma can kill you without proper and rapid treatment."

So, I allowed myself to be checked into the hospital and be monitored carefully. Doctors, interns, and specialists in respiratory and pulmonary disease filed in and out of my hospital room at various intervals all day and half the night.

I had plenty of time to think; many questions ran through my mind. Why was I here? Why had I created this traumatic event? I hadn't been in a hospital for asthma since I was eight years of age. Why now?

When I was finally discharged after two days, my entire body felt like a heavy, dense, piece of flesh that didn't belong to me. I was so tired and weak I could barely walk. My whole system felt polluted. My spirit was dense and joyless, although I was happy to be returning home.

For two days I had had some of the best medical care available. I talked with several doctors who were respiratory authorities. I was told that my asthma would be with me the rest of my life, but I was also reassured that it could be controlled with drugs and attention to some environmental precipitators. And, of course, the hospital and all the technological and medical expertise would always be available.

This was comforting on one level, but on another level I felt restless, and even angry. I felt I had lost control of my health. It was nice to have the security of a hospital, but did that mean I would always have to live and work near a hospital? Why did this whole incident happen to me in the first place?

Several days later, when I was at home and resting comfortably, it dawned on me that I had never been given a choice about my asthmatic condition. The questions kept rising into my consciousness. Was asthma really incurable? Would I be dependent for the rest of my life on modern medicine and technology to keep me comfortable and to rescue me when I had a major attack? Was it really true that I would have this disease the rest of my life? How did they know?

Even if they never knew of anybody who had cured their asthma, did that mean it wasn't possible? Were they trying to dampen unrealistic expectations I might have for myself, and protect me from experiencing a sense of failure? Did they have that right, and, more importantly, was I going to give them that right to decide what was best for me?

Several months after my hospitalization, and feeling somewhat discouraged by the traditional western approach, I decided to try two "alternative" treatments. I began working with a stress diffusionist who used a combined technique of body work to release stress and psychological therapy to uncover the origins of the stress, which in my case originated in my relationship with my father. My work with her continued over several years.

I was confronted time and again with an issue around authority, and a fear of trusting my intuitive (or, right brain) part of myself. Rather than seeking internal guidance, I had constantly sought external approval from authority figures, the earliest and most powerful being my father. My task in this life was to realign with my higher self, and allow my soul to express itself more completely. I would be learning who I was, and to joyfully and fully express that real self without fear of public disapproval.

During the same period, but for a much shorter, though intense, period, I felt drawn to work with an acupuncturist, whom I visited twice a week. He had been recommended by a colleague of mine who spoke glowingly of the pain relief work she had received. I knew I had to seek this person out for treatment.

I noticed improvement at times with both procedures, but nothing lasting, and certainly nothing that could be called a cure. I didn't want to focus on a cure but it was hard not to. I wanted to have proof to make my investment of time, money, and energy worthwhile. How did I know what I was doing was making a difference? With western medicine I usually got a quick bang for my buck, even if the relief was only temporary. But I was after something bigger, a long term healing.

I was learning to listen to my higher guidance for messages that came from within me. Usually, when I followed these messages, I found the path easy to follow. There was a feeling of things fitting together. This helped me to trust the intuitive feelings I had.

I find that when I am tuning into my higher self, I experience an unfolding which to me is symbolized by how easily I can get an appointment with someone. Also, I felt an easy kinship when first talking with the acupuncturist, and later during the treatments. And, even the fact that the treatments were covered by my insurance felt right. There was a sensing of things opening up which was accompanied by some symbols or signs confirming my feelings.

It was hard being patient and trusting that what I was doing in terms of healing would eventually manifest with physical results. I knew that healing had to take place on many other levels before the symptoms would show a shift on the physical level.

Over time I learned to accept this desire for a cure, but I also learned to relax more and to not become overly attached to the outcome. I was learning to become curious about, and enjoy the process of, treatment itself. I asked my doctors many questions, and read as much as I could understand about stress diffusion and acupuncture. I continued these treatments for about a year, when a part of me suggested I stop working with acupuncture and consider something new. I continued with stress diffusion.

Although somewhat discouraged by my earlier hospital experience, I felt it was time to return to western medicine and see if anything had been overlooked that would help me heal my asthma. A colleague of mine had written a book about his healing and treatment experiences with asthma, and had spoken favorably about certain medications that had done wonders for him. Perhaps I had not explored all the possibilities.

My family doctor suggested that I have an evaluation with the leading authority on asthma in the area. Although I had been warned that this doctor was very dogmatic and authoritative in his approach, I felt drawn to explore this line of treatment. Perhaps I would receive some new advice that would prove useful in obtaining a cure. Once again, some energy within me guided me to have this experience and it was not difficult to obtain a convenient appointment. At the very least, I felt I would gain an updated diagnosis and the latest medical information available.

Before I went to the office to be examined I was sent through the mail a detailed questionnaire to record my health history. Many of the questions had to do with my own observations of when I seemed to experience the worst asthma symptoms. I mentioned how cold weather, cut grass, pollen in the spring and fall, and running or exercising vigorously would set off an attack. But the number one trigger was stress. Ever since I was a child I had known that stress, good or bad, could set off an attack.

On the day of my appointment with the specialist, I had to wait only a very short time in a small, windowless room before being led into an even smaller room, where I was asked to breathe through a tube which was hooked to a monitor which would determine my lung capacity. I had done this before and knew the results could vary enormously depending on the procedure I used to blow into the tube. No instructions were offered, except to take a deep breath and blow as hard as I could for as long as I could.

My first try was a disaster, as I could see in the faces of the assistants around me. "Try again," they said. Now I was really nervous and tense. This last attempt was the most feeble of all. The nurse and the assistant said nothing. Oh, was I nervous!

They went over the drugs I had been using for my asthma. I mentioned the albuterol and the Chinese Ping Chuan pills my acupuncturist had given me. They stared at me, and told me they were sure the doctor would have something to say about the pills. Uh oh, I knew I was in trouble again. They asked me why I wasn't taking steroids, and I said I didn't want to take two medications. I was trying to cut down on medicine. Once again they told me the doctor would have something to say to me about that also.

I was relieved when they ushered me into another room which was still smaller than the previous one. This whole process of going to smaller and smaller spaces seemed to be a metaphor for the constriction going on in my lungs. A nurse pricked my arm with a string of needles to determine what my allergies were. After twenty minutes, she returned to record the red splotches on a sheet of paper listing all kinds of molds, grasses and dusts. She made several check marks before the categories; a few she said were marginal, but ones that the doctor should be made aware of.

I waited for close to an hour. I did find one piece of information to look at while waiting. It was a clipping from a *Newsweek* story on patients who didn't follow doctor's orders. There were a lot of statistics showing that patients could not be relied upon to do what was best for them, such as taking all their prescribed medications. The implication, it seemed, was that this was the reason why patients often didn't get well or stay well. Not too inspiring, I thought.

I was told the doctor was ready to see me. The moment was at hand. The tests were all in. I would now hear the results. I felt anxious.

The doctor sat behind a large desk with a stack of papers before him; presumably my test results and questionnaire.

Picking up one paper, which I could see was my questionnaire, he immediately told me that stress was not a relevant factor. He said, "Everyone has stress. Stress is what doctors tell patients when they don't know what else to say. This is not a consideration we deal with." I immediately knew I wasn't going to enjoy this. During the first minute of our conversation, he discredited my analysis as meaningless. I felt under attack. I fought to regain my center of calm and listen to his assessment. After all, in a half hour I would be out of here, and, more importantly, away from his authority. Then I would choose what I wanted to do.

He admitted that the medical profession doesn't know everything about asthma. This was the most humble statement he made. One thing he did know is that alternative medicine, including acupuncture and meditation, was in the category of what he called "groping theories." He always teaches his students these techniques are for people who don't want to take their medicine or follow doctor's orders. He said that acupuncture is not "logical, sensible, rational, scientific, practical, and will not give you what you want."

How did he know so much about acupuncture? Had he studied it? How did he know what I really wanted? He hadn't asked me anything; he was telling me. I was getting angry. He was discounting my self-healing efforts as worthless. Back off and listen, I said to myself.

But, he wasn't finished with his discourse on acupuncture. He began to compare the use of acupuncture to the massacre of the Bosnians by the Croatians. He couldn't condone in good conscience what was going on over there, just as he felt he had a moral responsibility to tell me what harm I was doing to myself.

I was having trouble following his line of reasoning. The only thing that was clear was that he didn't like acupuncture. He ended this part of the conversation by saying that he was quite liberal, but that using acupuncture was like "standing on your head and baying at the moon." I wondered what a Chinese doctor working with a five thousand year tradition of medicine and healing would have said to him. If he was smart, he would smile and walk away. Anything else would have been wasted effort.

At this point, the specialist pulled out the report on my allergic reactions based on tests done that morning. He discussed the importance of taking out carpets and rugs, if at all possible, and cleaning sheets regularly with hot water. All of this was because of the presence of a microscopic bug called a dust mite. In case I didn't get the message, he showed me what looked like a thousand-time enlarged, black and white photo of a frightening bug that looked like something out of one of those old monster movies. I was impressed. All I could do was to try to cut down my exposure to them as much as possible.

We talked about how to change my environment to rid ourselves of the pesky mite. I might use air filters, get rid of or, at least thoroughly clean, the rugs and drapes in my home. As he talked, I knew his suggestions were not too practical for my way of living. I could sense him sizing me up as one more patient who was either too stupid or too lazy to do what was in his best interest.

What seemed to be the answer for me, but wasn't being addressed, was how I could create two very healthy lungs so that all these *external* changes were unnecessary. Perhaps I was just being lazy, but it seemed to me that rather than rearrange the living environment, why not find out why the lungs were malfunctioning in the first place. I knew it would be futile to bring up the mind/body connection with this physician. So I decided to try to listen.

After lecturing me about my living environment, he turned to my use of the bronchodilator. Sometimes I would need to use it six or more times a day. This was to be supplemented by an additional steroid spray that would have longer term benefits. He told me it was essential that I use, on a regular basis, the new steroid spray so that I could cut down on the number of asthma attacks I have, and also the use of the albuterol spray. The albuterol gives relief, but does nothing for the underlying inflammation, and if used over many years, could cause permanent scar tissue to form on the lungs, leading to irreversible lung damage. Scary stuff, I thought.

The new steroid inhaler was an anti-inflammatant, and represented state of the art preventive therapy. There were supposedly no side effects from long term use except some hoarseness, and an occasional yeast infection which could be treated with other drugs. He stressed that if I didn't do this now, my lungs would lose all elasticity as I aged and I would be reduced to very little activity, with a lung capacity that barely sustained my life.

Several times he repeated what bad shape I was in, since I had only 41% lung capacity. I had heard this argument before, though not as dramatically. Even with all the evidence and authority of the medical establishment, I knew the last thing I wanted to do was to add another medication, although, presumably, I would need less of the albuterol. Sure it was safe, I thought, but only based on what we knew about its long-term effects to date.

A book I had read on the causes and treatment of asthma documented how what we think of today as a medical miracle can be tomorrow's poison, with unknown side effects showing up years later. Even the pills we take to help us may be poisoning us in other ways, such as through the dyes used to color the pills.

As I sat in his office, I found myself trusting this doctor less and less as he continued to lecture me. How could he discount what I knew to be the number one precipitator of my attacks, although certainly stress was not the explanation for all of them. He was so positive about what I should and should not do. I feel it's important for a doctor and patient to have a bond of trust for any treatment to be effective. I also felt that a patient had to experience a sense of involvement and self empowerment to be committed to working with the doctor to heal his or her diseased condition.

This doctor viewed me as a potentially disobedient child who had to be scared into following orders. Fear is only an effective motivator if the person inducing the fear is always present to keep reminding the person of their obligation. He would not be always present. As soon as I walked out of that office I would be in charge again, and my desire to reassert my own independence would lead me in the direction of non-compliance.

Nevertheless, I still wanted to learn as much as I could by this visit, however, I sensed the specialist was in a hurry and did not really want a dialogue.

Time was passing quickly and I was determined to ask my one overriding question about the main reason I had come to him in the first place. "Doctor, how can I cure my asthma and what is the probability of doing it?" He looked at me incredulously. "Your chances of curing your asthma are one in a thousand." He paused for a moment, looking right at me, and then, with a very authoritative voice, said, "No, your chances are less than one in ten thousand."

Well, that answered my question. He went on to tell me that he lectured to interns at the University of Vermont medical school about treating asthma, and then pointed to a row of books, volumes of them having to do with respiratory research and treatment, as if to underlie his authority for making this probability statement. Finally, to illustrate his point, he began inhaling and exhaling in rapid short puffs like someone who has just finished a marathon and is gasping for air. He said that would be my situation in a few years if I didn't follow his instructions.

Later that day, I reflected back on his proclamation about the possibility for a cure for asthma. Are most doctors afraid of arousing false hope? The way he responded made it sound hopeless. How different I might have felt had he said something like, "I don't know much about cures. Perhaps one in ten thousand have cured their condition. We don't know how to cure asthma, but obviously some people have." I got out my calculator. Given the one in ten thousand probability, and one in twenty Americans with asthma, means that approximately 1200 Americans have cured their asthma.

I also wondered how many people had cured their asthma, but never bothered to tell their doctor. It also struck me as more than coincidental, that I had met three former asthmatics. Their accounts were inspirational for me.

All my life I had had asthma, at least since I was eighteen months old. I am particularly sensitive to being around someone who has a cold for fear of the consequences if I should catch it. During one attack when I was very young, I was administered the last rites of the Catholic Church. My parents were convinced I was going to die.

Whenever I got a cold, I would often have an asthmatic complication, though never serious enough to require hospitalization. It also intensified after my divorce, when I began needing almost daily medication.

It was after my last hospitalization that I realized I had to choose whether to learn to live with this discomfort, relying on western medicine and medical monitoring the rest of my life, or to assume full responsibility and learn what it was here to teach me, and thus eliminate its purpose and perhaps also its presence.

In addition to working with acupuncture and stress diffusion, I joined the Transcendental Meditation Center and learned their form of meditation. I recited a mantra twice a day which was supposed to reduce stress and help me gain a greater inner and outer harmony in my life. I followed an Ayurvedic diet, took special herbal remedies, and used nose drops especially meant to enhance my breathing capacity. Day after day I affirmed to myself that I wished to cure my asthma.

Some days I was discouraged and some days elated. But, something told me never to give up, and to be open to whatever healing modality presented itself to me. Again and again, I felt drawn to certain healers and healing traditions without knowing what I could expect. I always had two goals in mind; 1) to heal my asthma; and, 2) to understand how it happened so I could teach others how they could heal themselves.

The first time I became aware that it was really possible was two weeks before my gall bladder operation, when the asthma seemed to diminish rapidly. I was obsessed and worried about the outcome of the surgery, however irrational it might now seem. I didn't sleep or eat well for weeks before the operation. The asthma was not of much interest to me. One evening, I noticed that I hadn't taken any asthma medication that day, and my lungs seemed to correct themselves when I normally would have used the spray. I reduced my medication intake 80 to 90% over several days. This was one of the most surprising and exciting discoveries during a period in my life when I was going through a great deal of fear and anxiety. Medical personnel I told seemed baffled by this outcome, but more surprisingly, didn't seem to care, either.

What I learned from Sir Garrod was that I was so focused on curing the gall bladder that the asthma literally moved aside. It seemed so much less life-threatening than the surgery, that I took my energy away from it, and, in a sense, I forgot its presence in my life. I detached from having to cure the asthma, and it was free to move away. "What resists persists," and I was no longer resisting.

I also noticed the asthma disappeared whenever I was involved in writing poetry, which can become a passion with me. I became so absorbed in the writing process that the asthma actually moved aside during the time I was writing.

Since I was only writing for short periods of time, the effect was not as pronounced as it was with the gall bladder surgery. However, the feeling was exactly the same during both the surgery and the writing situation. My lungs expanded, as though I had just taken my medication. In this case the body was somehow producing its own healing.

Both of these situations were major breakthroughs. I now knew that it was possible to affect this condition through my thought, my state of being. But, did I have to have surgery every time I wanted to heal my lungs? I found myself waiting almost another year before I experienced another change. Once again my medication was reduced by 80% to 90% of what I had been taking before the change.

What made this different is that there was no surgical crisis, nor did it happen only when I was writing. Although the consequence was quite dramatic, the causes were more subtle.

I began by using my bronchodilator *without* medication. Again and again I found that it usually had the same effect whether there was any medication present or not. This simple physical act seemed to trigger a healing response in my lungs.

On other occasions I would simply "talk" to my lungs and ask them if they could adjust without even the placebo. Often they said "yes," particularly if I was not under stress. On occasion they would say to take the medication and not "to test" them. In a stressful situation, I did not want to have to worry if I would begin to wheeze. And, there were times when I even felt drawn to using the steroid medication.

At other times, I would slowly test my lungs in circumstances where I normally used the medication, such as just before giving a presentation. The first time I did this before a major presentation, I was scared, and could feel signs of wheezing. Once I got over the initial fear, and involved in my work the wheezing subsided. It was one more major triumph and was much easier to do the next time.

I always took the medication whenever I was about to engage in a brisk walk in cold weather, or engage in a vigorous activity, such as tennis. I experimented. When it got below zero and the wind chill made the temperature a lot lower, I found I always had to use the real medication. However, sometimes I could use the placebo if the weather was a little warmer. Once, I didn't make it completely through a vigorous errand without needing the placebo. The next time I didn't need even that. Each little triumph encouraged me to take the next step. I was learning about my disease and not automatically reacting with medication.

For years I had never gone to bed without taking the medication first. I would almost always wake up during the night needing it. Then I began to experiment by going to bed some nights without taking it. Occasionally I would wake up; sometimes the placebo worked, and sometimes I needed the real medication. There was no predictable pattern, which, in itself, was a major change. A few times I went through the entire night without needing any medication.

I found myself appreciating my lungs and my asthma more than I ever had. Each little triumph increased my self esteem, and I experienced less of a sense of failure when I had to resort to using medication. It was no longer an "all or nothing" experience.

The cure was secondary to the learning process going on between my consciousness and my body. I was becoming aware of how we create obstacles to overcome so we can learn and enhance our feelings of self worth. Sometimes I got very excited, and wanted to tell my friends of my triumphs.

However, this act of going public created some of my greatest fears, and perhaps actually slowed down my healing process. I was terribly afraid of letting anyone know of my successes, and even waited several weeks before reluctantly telling one of my best friends. I worried about letting my friends down if I didn't progress fast enough. It was an old issue of mine about taking on responsibility for other people's happiness.

How did I know that the asthma wouldn't come back to the point where I would have to return to the full use of the medication? I would be a failure to myself. I was getting attached again to the concept of the cure. I was battling old habits.

I still wanted to know more about why I had created the asthma in the first place, and why I had put myself through so many healing modalities and treatments. For someone with a linear, rational mind, it was hard to see why I wasn't just being a dilettante in search of some magic bullet. Even if I did heal the asthma, how would I know which of the many treatments I had undergone was the key ingredient? My mind was still looking for that one treatment which could be isolated as the catalyst.

Sometimes when I take my medication, I tend to see it as a reminder of my own inability to heal myself, and I realize that each time I focus on this experience as being a "failure," I give energy to the concept, and it simply reinforces and prolongs the asthma.

I try to appreciate the general improvement in my health. I have far fewer colds than I used to (my most severe asthma attacks used to grow out of colds or flu). Although eliminating asthma is still my ultimate goal, I am grateful for the improvement. I try not to judge my progress on the basis of whether or not there is a complete cure.

Gradually I am learning a new strategy that isn't based on control and goal attainment. I realize my asthma has served me well for many years, including obtaining sympathy from a father who had difficulty expressing love. Asthma has become a long-standing habit that is very much a part of my psyche and body. My physical being has gotten used to taking medication, and probably wonders what life would be like without it. Even a habit we want to get rid of provides a known security.

For now, I am grateful for any decreases in the medication, for however long it lasts, and I will continue to put out my intent to reduce the medication still further for longer periods of time and under even more stressful conditions. Until it does leave, I will continue to perceive my asthma as a challenging opportunity to learn more about myself, my potential to heal, and how I might serve by helping others wake up to their own inner wisdom and healing abilities.

———•••••———

Tom was involved in a struggle to find out a positive aspect about his asthma. Reaching the goal became an obsession with him. Instead of focusing on and appreciating the intervals he did not need the medication, he saw taking medication as a sign of failure. Using the medication indicated to him he had experienced a setback in reaching his goal. He knew his impatience was getting in the way, and at the same time he realized he wanted to immediately receive patience.

It is not a matter of giving up the desire for a certain healing outcome, but it is necessary to give up managing and constantly measuring the process. Tom needed to reduce his constant attention on the goal, and create a space so healing could take place. He was not required to lose sight of the goal, but he did need to relax so the healing would occur. He knew that once he took the energy away from the illness, such as happened when he had been focused on the surgery or writing poetry, he created a healing space. T o do this required a major expansion in Tom's beliefs. He did not reject allopathic medicine, but included a new belief system based on mind power and self healing in his treatment. In some cases he had to trust these new beliefs over the opinions of some major medical authorities.

In addition, Tom chose to change his beliefs by taking small steps over a period of time. There is no reason that he had to embrace a new set of beliefs immediately, but rather, he could phase in the new principles over time, retaining the old belief system for as long as it proved useful and provided needed comfort.

He bounced back and forth between wanting to take control of the process and to succeed at being cured, while simultaneously taking pleasure in all the many healing experiences and lessons he was drawing to himself. Even though he was very conscious of what to do, and very much aware of the spiritual principles, it was different from actually being able to do it. It was one thing to understand the concepts and another to practice them.

During his conversations with Sir Garrod, Sananda and McDermott, Tom was told again and again that he was too intently focused on the goal and too concerned with identifying the specifics for a cure, rather than on allowing the body to heal itself. They reminded him that the greatest reduction in the asthma occurred when his consciousness was preoccupied with the upcoming surgery, and he should remember this. He let go simply because he had a more significant, overriding situation to pay attention to. His higher self knew what path he needed to take for the desired outcome, and it was most important to learn to allow and trust where it was guiding him. Sir Garrod reminded him that "all obstacles and challenges you experience in your life, including your asthma, are for purposes of learning."

McDermott pointed out that the asthma presented an opportunity for him to learn to trust his inner guidance. "You have been learning how to tune into your inner or higher wisdom as it guides you from treatment to treatment. There is a concept you are familiar with called 'going with the flow.' It means to have a clear goal in mind, but to hold onto the goal lightly, and to flow with the experiences that arise during the process of realizing the goal. In this flow of experience there is only the confidence of all things unfolding perfectly all the time with no judgment. All potential that is of the highest for you will be ever moving into position. If you simply allow your longings to guide you and not judge, and to realize there is nothing more to do but listen and follow your path, then you will always be working on whatever truth you are to work on at any given moment."

McDermott emphasized that beyond that conscious mind "is a much larger mind of which you are not normally conscious. It is from this larger mind that interests and goals, and the path to achieving those desires, emerge into your conscious mind. You have been losing the need to control. You are beginning to understand there is a wise part of the self that is orchestrating your experiences, so you can relax and simply allow things to move into place.

"You have been learning that you can trust, and that once you affirm something, everything that happens is preparing you to have it. You have been learning that everything that happens is manifesting for you in the perfect time and in the perfect way. Since you will get what you ask for, it is only necessary that you be sure and clear on what you really want."

A key lesson for Tom was to learn to follow his inner guidance, and not be automatically persuaded by external medical authorities. Sir Garrod told us our culture puts a great deal of trust in medical technology and expertise, which makes it difficult to go against such authority. Each of us must learn to take responsibility for our own healing. This can include, but need not be limited to, traditional western medicine.

Often, medical researchers don't know what the long-range side effects a treatment may have. Today's wonder drug may have negative effects in the long-term. Doctors do not always know if their tests are accurate. Science is couched in probabilities, and medicine is an inexact science. If the probabilities say an individual should benefit from a specific treatment, how do doctors know that person isn't an exception and may actually be harmed by that particular therapy? Even aspirin isn't safe for everyone, and can have deleterious consequences for people with ulcers and children with certain flu-like symptoms. Will, motivation, and beliefs are too frequently overlooked by the medical profession as being able to influence a person's health and well-being.

Betty: Learning to Trust Yourself

Doctors told Betty she was hypothyroid, a condition which would necessitate she be on medication the rest of her life. The diagnosis was based upon blood tests, and the symptoms she had were very different from those the doctors said she should be experiencing. She felt she was hyperthyroid, and not hypothyroid as diagnosed.

———————

In essence, the blood test contradicted what was going on inside of me. Tests were repeated but the doctors kept coming up with the same diagnosis. I reminded my doctor that my symptoms certainly did not support the diagnosis, and, in fact, contradicted it. So she agreed to do the test again. The results were even more dramatically hypothyroid. I began taking the medication, although I still felt the diagnosis was wrong.

I took the medication for three months with no real change in my symptoms. The blood tests were repeated, and showed that the thyroid level was still very low. My medication dosage was increased. My gut feeling continued to be that the diagnosis was wrong and I should not take the medication, but I continued because I had been warned that it was dangerous to play around with thyroid medication, and I couldn't imagine ignoring blood test results.

I sought a second opinion. This doctor took one look at me and said "you aren't hypothyroid." I felt relieved. We did more blood tests, and the results were still hypothyroid. The doctor couldn't explain it, but felt the tests could not be ignored. She switched the type of thyroid supplement I was to take, and I began a series of treatments with her trying to discover the emotional source of the problem in my body. I was ready to try anything. What a time of wonder and learning!

At one point I sought an opinion from an endocrinologist, who had no explanation for the fact that my symptoms contradicted the blood test. What bothered me most was that she wasn't even interested in wondering why that might be the case. Her advice was to take the medication and repeat the tests to regulate the amount of medication.

After several years, I finally got up the courage to tell my doctor that I couldn't keep ignoring my gut feeling that taking the medication was wrong. I didn't care what the test results were. They never corresponded with how I was feeling and I had learned that the longer you take thyroid medication, the more your body depends on it.

At first she balked at the idea, because as an M.D. it was difficult for her to agree to drop the treatment despite blood test results. Then she realized that one of the major issues we kept coming across in our work together was *speaking my truth*. She couldn't ask me to continue ignoring my strong feelings. I burst into tears because I was so grateful to be told I should follow my feelings, and I would have her medical support if I needed help.

It took more than a year to taper off the medication, feeling better and stronger all the time. It has been six months now since I took any thyroid supplement. When I try to see why I brought this lesson to myself (I would never have been tested, had I not asked to be tested), I now see that my body was trying to get my attention. Would I have done all the healing, reading, and thinking I did had it not been for the physical issues? Through this I learned that this condition was a bodily manifestation of not taking care of myself or loving myself. So often my life revolved around the needs of others, usually not to either their benefit or mine, and this would exhaust me.

Now I have developed a new feeling, kind of in the pit of my stomach, which shows up whenever I am overextending myself. This tells me to back off and take care of myself, or be prepared for another bout of that overwhelming fatigue. I find this new tool, or gauge, gets triggered sooner and sooner before I get really fatigued. I am working toward the day when I won't even need this bodily warning to get me to respect my own needs. But now it is very useful.

I may never know what was really going on with my body, hypo- or hyperthyroidism, or something else all together, but it forced me to look at my care taking propensity, and it got me to learn to trust my own gut feelings and self healing abilities despite medical evidence to the contrary. When I feel fatigue now, which I seldom do, I don't resent my body for causing me discomfort. I know it is working on my behalf to keep me taking care of myself. How loud and painful the signal gets is up to me, and my response increasingly is to quieter gentler signals.

The whole experience has opened my inner senses. My goal is to get ever better at paying attention to those senses and acting on them, so that my lessons can be learned as gently as possible.

Conclusion

A major lesson that Tom and Betty both learned revolved around the importance of treating information based solely on medical authority and expertise with some caution. It is not a case of rejecting such medical counseling or advice, but rather learning to take responsibility for one's own healing process.

Tom and Betty's choice to use alternative healing methods does not suggest that traditional medical treatment should be overlooked. The idea is to include other methods of healing in order to expand the number of tools available for use. So often we overvalue traditional medical knowledge, and undervalue our own intuitive expertise. We need a balance. The more resources at our disposal, the better equipped we are to combat the problems challenging us.

Betty's willingness to trust her inner senses served as an inspiration for many in the manifestation group as she chose to follow her intuitive guidance instead of the advice offered by traditional medicine. So often it seems easier to relinquish our power to the medical authorities and deny our own inner wisdom. Betty was courageous enough to give priority to her own bodily wisdom, and to develop an inner mechanism to signal when her old patterns around care taking were emerging. She honored herself and her body, and no longer required the thyroid condition to serve as an external manifestation of lack of self love to attract her attention.

Tom's intuitive guidance seemed like a combination of "joyous feeling" and "effortless opportunity." For example, when he felt drawn to have a stress diffusion session, a cancellation would present itself at a time when he was free to go. When his colleague mentioned how much she liked her acupuncturist, he felt an urge to call and make an appointment because the connection felt right. The feeling of rightness and the opportunity easily came together.

Betty had a gut feeling that the medical diagnosis was wrong. Moreover, the symptoms were completely at odds with what she was supposed to be experiencing. The medical authorities were wedded to the technical tests. But Betty was able, over time and after much frustration, to honor her own authority, and choose a different direction.

Tom received an inspirational analysis of his intuitive process from Sir Garrod. "When you decided to cure your asthma, your mind developed a clear goal around a healthy set of lungs. You were clear in your intent and committed your will to the end of creating healthy lungs. At that point, you released the intent, trusting the soul to provide the necessary experiences that would cure the disease. The higher self, in a sense, went out in all directions and magnetized to you the coincidences, people, and events that create what you wanted; a healthy set of lungs. This happened beyond the level of the mind. You followed your inner urgings and guidance to join this flow, and this led you to all the healers and healing that could assist your own healing process.

"You came to understand that once you put something out that you wished to experience, you could not judge that which unfolded because you could not understand the wholeness of what you were working with. Setting a goal and measuring the process are two different things. You had to know that with every experience you were getting to where you wanted to go. You did have doubts but not enough to stop your process."

Allowing was a key theme for Tom, as well. His perception of his bronchitis changed from resistance, to allowing. His goal of being healthy did not change, but he no longer resisted the process. He trusted that his process was achieving his goal, even if this meant he continued to have the illness. He took his attachment and attention away from the illness, and focused instead on healing and health. When he gave up trying to control the illness, it was free to leave him; over a series of months, it did.

When Tom began his process, he had considerable attachment to the goal of cure, and was in constant measurement of any progress. When he was able to give up the monitoring and judgment of the process, such as during the time before his surgery, the asthma seemed to disappear. He learned that progress is a not a measure of self worth.

It takes courage to trust inner guidance when the consequences of disobedience of authority can very well have life or death consequences. Tom cannot be certain that by not taking the steroid medication recommended by the doctor he won't have a detrimental outcome twenty or thirty years in the future. Nor can he be sure that taking it wouldn't prove to be detrimental, as medical scientists continue to learn more about the long-term consequences of this medication. All he can do is follow his conscience during the present, trust the choice made as one coming from his inner guidance, and then become an observer of what happens.

The key is to connect with the guidance offered through the higher self. There is no blanket solution or single answer. Someone else might heal their bronchitis, thyroid, or asthma by following a very different process from those used by the individuals in this chapter. Still others may not totally cure their illnesses, but attain a whole new state of improvement in their health and attitude. Nor is there any reason not to take small steps. Become your own experimenter, and watch for what seems to be working. Become a master observer of yourself. No one can possibly know as much about you as you!

Chapter 6

Relationships

In the previous chapter, the persons relating their stories said they were learning to believe and *trust* their inner guidance to *allow* healing to unfold. Through the various diseases and discomforts they experienced, they learned of internal attitudes, beliefs and lessons which were being projected or mirrored externally in their bodies.

Illness is not the only manifestation of internal beliefs or lessons; relationships with other people can also reflect those beliefs and afford an opportunity for learning. According to Sir Garrod, relationships, particularly those of a romantic nature, are where we do some of our most intensive study. An individual may become a teacher and mirror for the other in a relationship, since issues often tend to be projected onto the other person.

Major issues in relationships are similar to those encountered when dealing with illness, and often center around themes of control, self-responsibility, acceptance, and allowance. Just as our body may reflect a feeling of low self worth, an abusive partner may be a projected manifestation of how poorly we view ourselves. The need to control a romantic partner may be a reflection of our own inability to give ourselves the love that we demand.

It is possible for these projections to become opportunities for healing, which, in turn, can result in attracting wholesome relationships, just as the process resulted in better health for Betty and Tom.

If we accept responsibility for our feelings, actions, and the way we react, we have an opportunity to heal them and create greater peace and harmony in our relationships. If we continue to project our attitudes onto someone else, we will continue to recreate uncomfortable circumstances until we pay attention.

When relationships end, there is often great sadness and loss of self-esteem. Frequently, there is anger, bitterness, and fault-finding. It is easy, and almost expected in our society, to resort to blame and accusation. We feel hurt, wounded, and tend to judge either ourselves or our ex-partner for the breakup.

But the opportunity for a new start is also present if the individuals choose to view the change in the relationship as just that—change, an opportunity to progress. Once again, it is not the breakup in a relationship that causes the sadness and trauma, it is the way we choose to perceive the experience that carries significance.

The focus in one set of choices may be external and future-oriented. "My happiness is dependent on your changing your behavior," is often stated. The other person is expected to change their behavior to meet our needs.

The alternative choice is to focus on the moment, live in the present, and trust the experiences to unfold. Acceptance and non-judgment become major themes which define interaction.

Following this second choice, we see that relationships include a lot of learning about ourselves and our partners. When we feel uncomfortable with something our partner does, we may find this to be simply a projection of something we do not accept in ourselves, and by recognizing this, we are presented with an opportunity to heal. We, as partners, become teachers for each other.

We always accept full responsibility for our behavior. No matter what our partner says or does, we have the choice of how to respond; what action to take.

Mary's Story

The first account is from Mary, who has been divorced for seven years, and in and out of several relationships during that time. None were serious, except for the one she describes here. Mary is very conscious of the value of using spiritual principles, and finds them to be a great source of comfort and guidance. She used the principle of acceptance around her response to a recent promotion opportunity. This turned out to be a much easier experience than accepting the break up with her lover. Both are presented to compare her responses.

The Job

A new position with a substantial increase in salary opened up for Mary. She was reasonably confident that she would be offered the position, and had the support of her colleagues over an outside candidate. When she was told she didn't get the job, she was surprised by how relieved she felt, and the fact that her colleagues were considerably angrier about her rejection than she was.

I had said to myself that whatever happens will tell me where to go and what to do. I temporarily got caught up in the socially desirable objective of a more prestigious position and more money. I had the backing of all the major administrative factions, as well as all the people who would be reporting to me. At first, I reasoned that by not getting the new position, it meant that I should begin right away along the riskier path of starting my own business. And, I could see that had I gotten that new position, I would have had no time to put into my dream project of starting my own business. I also might have felt hesitant to leave the new position after only a couple of years.

But, when I applied for the management position, something even better happened that I sensed all along, but couldn't really see. My colleagues just couldn't understand why I wasn't angrier with the decision. Somehow I knew it wasn't right for me—at least not at that time.

———•◦••◦•———

What Mary could not see at the time was the perfection of the manifestations of the third kind which she was creating for her learning process. First of all, her new manager provided her with a job environment that Mary thought was available to her only through a higher management position. And, secondly, working with her new boss was also preparing her with the necessary personal, social, and business skills that were necessary to implement her dream of having a business of her own.

———•◦••◦•———

With my new manager I have freedoms, benefits, and appropriate challenges I never would have had had I gotten the position instead of her. I originally thought I had to be the manager to get what I wanted. I now see the opposite would have happened. My new boss can make decisions I never could have [made] as an insider. I would have had enormous doubts about myself as the head of the office. I would be constantly worrying about whether I had made the right decision. Instead, she supports me in my present position, and has helped me make decisions that both empower me and help me empower those who report to me. She is a wonderful role model.

The person who got the job over me is someone I love to work for. We support each other's growth. I can go to her when I have a problem and ask, 'what have I got to learn from this?' She helps me see my issues, and I can help her see hers. We work together to come up with positive win-win solutions. She won't let any of us get away with complaining.

When my staff reports to me now, thanks to my manager's support, I no longer listen to their complaints and take them on as my problems. I tell them not to complain, but rather ask them what they can come up with to solve their problem. In the past I tended to take on all their problems and would stress out. Now I ask them to lighten up. I support their solutions wherever possible, and encourage them to take responsibility for their stuff. Much of this I have been learning by working with my new boss. She helps me come up with solutions so I don't have to take on everyone's burdens. I couldn't imagine how easy it would be.

Furthermore, without all the responsibilities the new management position would have entailed, I have time to heal myself on a lot of levels. I am healing issues around substance abuse, a knee that needed surgery, depression, and being overweight. I needed time to put into myself, and keeping my old job with a supportive manager gives me enough of a challenge, and time to heal and grow with limited stress.

I feel like I am growing in my position and gaining the skills I will need when I run my own business. I know I won't be here forever, but without the skills I am getting now, I doubt I would have done as well as I will. I can also see how an inheritance that I am entitled to, but keeps getting held up in the courts, will come through just when I am ready for it. My potential business partner is learning complementary skills at another job. My path is clearly unfolding before me.

It is funny that every time I think I know the path to get to my goal something happens that, at first, looks like it is hindering me. I can see how I am getting there, but it is not the way I thought. You can't control the path. Just when you think you know how to get there, the universe will say, "You'll get where you want to go but not on your terms."

It was not as easy for Mary to trust higher guidance with a romantic relationship. It might seem that if we trust the universe and apply higher spiritual principles to help us understand a decision, such as getting turned down for a promotion, that we could apply the same principles equally easily to all major decisions. This is not always, or even often, the case. Whereas Mary sensed very early that the promotion might not be what she really wanted, it took her longer to understand why a much desired relationship was not in her best interests.

The Romantic Partner

While on a trip to Central America, Mary met a man she felt was the soul mate of her dreams. They spent six-weeks together in an idyllic romance, and she was positive this relationship would last much longer after they returned to the United States.

Life was so magical when I was with him. I was aware that when he was with me, I tended to focus entirely on him and would cut back on my time with others. Even when he wasn't there, all I could do was think about the times we had together, and then anticipate the time we would be together again. How many times I replayed that last kiss just before he departed. I would remind myself that it would not be long before he would be in my arms again.

Shortly after I returned to Vermont my dream came to a terrible, shattering end. I did not know he had been seeing another woman at the same time he had been seeing me. He lived four hours away in Boston, and would see me on weekends and her during the week. Somehow he kept us both unaware of the other. Eventually guilt, and perhaps the strain of commuting, got to him and he knew he had to make a choice. Unfortunately for me, he chose her. At that point I was not saying that there must be some wonderful outcome, like the way the job situation had evolved so nicely.

I was furious. I felt betrayed...a fall guy. I was a mess when he told me what happened. I wanted to say, "How come you get to be happy with someone while I end up being alone again!" I had told him many times when we were together in Nicaragua not to get involved with me unless he would stick with me. I wanted a committed relationship, which he did make, but it was not with me. My thoughts shouted to him, "How could you date me and another woman, and not tell me? Don't you know you broke my heart!?"

And, of course, he still wanted to be my friend. So he could free himself of guilt, he would be my friend. "No Way!" I said. "You don't get to have your lovely relationship, and be rid of your guilt, too. Saying we were so similar and it was such a hard decision for you doesn't make it any easier. You waited until you had a sure thing with this other woman. You should have let me go earlier. I was to be the fall guy if it didn't work out with her. Thanks a lot!"

I knew he was feeling horrible, but, the fact is, he had his dream to go back to. On some level I knew he was doing the right thing for himself. He was going with his heart and feelings. But why couldn't they have led him to me over her? I was mad at the universe. I deserved better treatment. I was not open to hearing about some vague higher purpose, or returning to my proper path, at the time I was mourning this deep loss.

People were reacting to me as if I should feel the way they felt, and in some cases I did. It is hard to hurt so much without blame. I hurt because he left. My ego was feeling hurt. My feminist friends were angry with him even more than I was. I found myself dealing with my friends' hurt as much as my own.

I felt victimized by the situation. I screamed out at the universe to tell me what this was all about. I felt so strongly how the world did not support me in letting it go. People who said they understood, and wanted me to recognize it was for some higher purpose, did not understand, I thought. In fact, the most helpful people were those who said nothing at all. They were very non-judgmental people and showed they were there for me, but basically let me go through my own stuff and respected me for however I went about it.

Gradually, as I grieved for my loss, I was able to begin to see there was something in this experience for me. I knew I could only be a victim if I chose to be one. It had become increasingly clear that I would have done almost anything he wanted to preserve the relationship. My date book was packed with appointments and time and energy directed toward being with him. My focus on him was unbalanced, with no time for other things in my life, including pursuing my own dream of having my own business. I wondered if he would be jealous of my dream.

So often I found that when I was in a romantic relationship I shut out other people. I found myself giving up energy to other people. I find my best relationships with women are when I am not in a relationship with a man. I place too much importance on romance and the relationship itself. I am willing to bend everything in my life for the right relationship.

It was a pattern I had had in my former marriage. I was married to an abusive husband who had complete control over me. I gave away control no matter what he did. He didn't even have to hit me to get me to obey. Although no longer attracting abusive relationships, I was attracting partners to me to remind me of this old controlling pattern, so that I could heal it and be true to my own path.

It is becoming all right [with me] if there is no relationship in my life. Until now I never really believed this. It was an intellectual concept. Now I feel it. I can't honestly say I still don't harbor some feelings of bad will toward my former lover. Healing is not an overnight phenomena. I'm still waiting for this guy to recognize what he has given up by choosing her over me. I recognize these are games I am playing with my ego. There are still some deep hurts, and part of me wishes I would get past them, because my defenses are pretty high now. But that is where I am at the moment.

My path requires me to go it alone, at least as long as being in a relationship requires me to sacrifice my dream. Perhaps when I have fully learned this, I will attract someone who will also support me. I can begin to see how the relationship would likely tie me down and take me further away from my dream. Not being sidetracked with any of these situations was in my own best interest. Perhaps the relationship was the hardest to see because of the deep emotional healing required of me. At the moment, I do not have the dream in hand, but I can see it clearly again without distractions. Should new distractions come along, I believe I will be better able to recognize them before they get to the point of frustration, confusion and even pain."

————————

Mary had a difficult time applying spiritual principles when in great pain caused by a broken relationship. In fact, the people who reminded her of the larger lessons and growth this experience was bringing to her, were not perceived by her as helping her heal. She chose to be angry and to grieve. She felt victimized.

Although we may want to move beyond the victim consciousness, it is still important to acknowledge its presence; it serves to protect us from strong feelings of rejection. We may interpret being jilted as a sign there is something fundamentally wrong with us, because we are not the preferred love object of the one we love. Since we tend to seek confirmation of our self-worth from external sources, particularly through significant others, finding fault with the person who has rejected us protects our self esteem.

Following the rejection, we may find it easier to accept responsibility for the experience with the passage of time. We may be able to say to ourselves, "This experience is fearful for me. It brings up issues I would rather not face. It makes me afraid I will never have what I want." This response replaces the question, "How could you do this to me?" which comes from a place of fear.

The irony is that if we could accept this situation as part of a larger plan that is bringing the relationship we desire, it would probably materialize much more rapidly. This entails forgiveness of self, as well as forgiving the person who had done the rejecting. The difficulty encountered is that the entire process cannot be seen from the perspective of our limited consciousness.

Over time, Mary did begin to see how this relationship was another step in her healing. She had grown beyond abusive relationships, but still retained issues around control and the surrender of self when in romantic relationships. A part of her was ready to grow beyond this, even though it was painful.

Her story illustrates how attachment and neediness bring what we are most afraid of. Mary feared she would be rejected, and could not let go of the need to control her relationship. That need may have precipitated the outcome. She resisted the possibility that the relationship could dissolve. What we resist persists, and she manifested what she was most afraid of happening.

Near the end of her account, Mary began to see how the dream to own her own business might easily have been sidetracked by a relationship which consumed so much of her attention and energy. She wanted to learn how to be in a liaison without totally losing herself. She was also able to compare how she reacted to this situation with the response she had when the job promotion fell through, even though the emotional pain of a broken romance was so much greater.

Mary needed to honor her disappointment and grief before she could move forward, and see how she had been distracted from her true goals. She also was beginning to realize that she needed to confront and heal personal issues before she could enjoy a healthy relationship. It started with recognizing her boyfriend's role as a teacher of what those issues were. She found it is possible to be angry and grieve, while learning and growing at the same time.

In retrospect, Mary realizes that the breakup of her romance has helped her just as much as being bypassed for the promotion benefited her. "I am glad we aren't together," she says. "He would have held back my growth. He's still caught up with defining himself by how others see him. I would have gotten frustrated and wanted him to grow at my pace. We would not have appreciated each other as much.

"As I look back I have no regrets even though it was painful. I learned about detachment, and not to be so willing to alter my life for someone else."

Less than a year after the romance had ended, Mary was attracted to a newly-divorced man who was very scared of entering into any kind of a commitment. She realized this relationship was an opportunity for her to learn to be in what she called a "romantic friendship," with psychological and sexual intimacy, but no expectations about the future of the relationship. During her previous relationship, she was constantly projecting into the future. Although unsettling and different, she felt this experience was very important for her as another step toward the committed relationship she really desired. The fragility of the relationship made her uncomfortable, yet she welcomed the challenge to be solid and secure in herself, as well as offering a safe haven for her lover to learn to open to his heart.

The key was to be in such an intimate relationship without expectation. Could she feel comfortable allowing him to express himself and fully explore his potential, even if that meant he had dated other women, and quite possibly would eventually leave her? Did it matter if they didn't see each other, or even phone, for days at a time? Could she just enjoy the time they spent together without becoming attached to the outcome? She wasn't sure, but she affirmed that if it became too difficult, "I will end the romantic part of the relationship. I am not going to lose his friendship."

"I really enjoy the time I'm with Malcolm. I also know if I start projecting things into the future, it will drive him away. If I take one day at a time and leave myself open to whatever else is out there, I will never be disappointed. This attitude seems to draw him closer to me. He's really teaching me about non-attachment. It is almost like bio-feedback; every time I start getting dependent on him, he goes away. The minute my neediness comes out, he is gone. He forces me to be healthy. When I don't need to have him in my life, he is there.

I won't limit my possibilities. I know I need to have lots of people meeting my needs if I am not to be attached to someone. I'm not looking for an exclusive relationship, or at least I'm not planning on it. I don't need a relationship to make me happy.

With my former lover, I couldn't eat or sleep for weeks worrying about the relationship. With Malcolm, I'm learning not to plan ahead. It isn't good for me to attach happiness to my expectations. He's teaching me spontaneity, and not to put my happiness in someone else's hands. I think I'm also learning that if someone else comes along for him, that it is not a rejection of me. It is simply another choice for new learning."

What is striking to the outside observer is how aware Mary has become of what she is experiencing in her relationships. She has accepted that she does a lot of her most important learning during her relationships with men. She courageously jumped into a new relationship, but with both eyes open. This liaison offered her a new challenge; a new opportunity. She knows this affords a very important lesson of healing around neediness and detachment, and willingly she has been allowing it to emerge into her experience and consciousness.

Mark's Story

Mark had been married seventeen years when his wife told him she wanted a divorce. Although their marriage had little excitement, it was a comfortable arrangement and, at first, Mark couldn't understand why she would want to create turmoil. His wife said she felt a marriage should have more vitality and growth...and challenge. She also let him know he wasn't emotionally sensitive to her need for love and affection. Mark was satisfied with their arrangement. He thought he had been a very supportive husband and the marriage was fine the way it was. The divorce toppled his whole foundation, and he felt sad, lonely, and empty.

Mark didn't know it, but the dissolution of his marriage was the beginning of a journey of self-discovery and healing which probably would not have evolved had he remained married. In contrast to Mary, he felt little rage or resentment. Loneliness and sadness were present with great intensity; particularly for the first six months after they separated. Although he was not aware at the time, because of anger and bitterness creating an attachment to the past, new opportunities were on his horizon.

By agreeing to the divorce, Mark created an opening to develop the emotional and expressive side of himself. Although his path was confusing, he began to construct a new foundation, heal, and release a great deal of repressed emotion. A ten year period of trying to achieve an ideal relationship followed. What on the surface seemed to be a series of failed relationships, turned out to be the very building blocks of what he desired.

———•◦•——

"As far as divorces go, mine was a good divorce. Although for months I experienced great loneliness and sadness after the separation, I can't say I ever doubted the correctness of the decision, even though it was she who initiated the divorce. Clearly, she had seen before I did that our marriage had deteriorated into nothing more than a congenial practical arrangement.

She wanted more than this, and, although I was afraid to admit it, I did, too. The difference was that I didn't know what "the more" that I wanted was. What would happen to me if we separated? Better to remain in a comfortable, but stable (if not a deeply satisfying) loving relationship. The unknown of being alone was much too frightening to even contemplate.

I thought I was a very supportive spouse. I did my share of the housework, earned half the income, equally shared in the child care, and supported her as she pursued her career. What more could she want from me?

During joint counseling, she told the psychiatrists that I was unemotional and unaffectionate. She pointed out I never cried openly when our daughter died forty-eight hours after she was born, or reassured my wife of my love for her, or empathized with her sadness, or hugged her spontaneously. In my defense, I could only recount the number of times I had done the dishes, supported her travel, or taken care of the children so she could advance professionally.

Emotionally, she wanted more from me than I thought I was capable of giving. How could I learn to hug her spontaneously, or reassure her I cared about her? I felt hemmed in. I didn't have the tools to give her the emotional and empathic support and understanding she was demanding from me when I didn't know how to give this to myself. When the counselors kept asking me what I wanted from my wife, all I could say was that I wanted her to be happy. Did I have no needs of my own?

Within a few months of my separation, I was attracted to a fellow worker in my department. I was so emotionally needy at that time that I obsessed about her constantly, and fantasized about intimate, romantic conversations and sexual encounters with her. I used to walk past her home at night, hoping to catch a glimpse of her, or accidentally running into her, so that I could talk to her. A luncheon engagement was something to look forward to with great anticipation.

My ex-wife was about to be remarried. I envied her. Where was my mate? How could I end the pain of loneliness and emptiness? The "fix" was to remarry as soon as possible.

Outwardly, and inwardly, my business associate appeared to be an excellent partner. She was attractive, my regular tennis partner, did the same kind of work as I, was bright, sensitive, loving, and had another business on the side which I also found interesting. Our music interests were similar, and, overall, anyone could tell we were congenial together. I received a great deal of acceptance from her, even though she teased me a lot (it was always in good fun). I was sure fate had destined this relationship; we were a perfect match.

I did, however, have trouble understanding why she kept introducing me to her best female friends and encouraging me to date them. I thought maybe she just wanted me to like her friends. Unfortunately, I learned something from those friends that made me uneasy. In fact, I denied it to myself for a long time. They kept telling me she preferred women, and that she was gay. At first, I attributed this to jealousy on their part. But, as time went on, and more and more people (some of whom I was not dating) said the same thing, it became harder to ignore. Finally, I confronted her directly and she told me the truth. She was very angry at the friends who had violated her trust, and showed little sympathy with my anguish about this revelation, because she was not ready to reveal her sexual preference to the straight community. She had major fears about coming out centering around acceptance by friends in the straight community, her job, and, most of all, her parents who expected her to marry.

If that wasn't enough, after finally accepting this disappointment, and without knowing it, I was later attracted to her new partner; a woman with two sons who had recently divorced. Because this woman had been married almost as long as I had been, and also had children, it never occurred to me she could be gay. I felt she would be a great romantic partner, since we shared much in common, including children. It was only after considerable time had passed and we had enjoyed each other's company that she told me she, too, was gay. She didn't want to tell me, because she didn't want to lose my friendship. For the second time in less than a year, I experienced frustration. I felt deceived, manipulated, angry, and very confused. Were all women secretly gay? I couldn't believe what was happening. What was wrong with my selection process?

There were two other gay women I was attracted to. I was really beginning to think the only unmarried women left in my age group were gay. It was easier to assume that every woman I was attracted to was gay; at least until I found out otherwise. Eventually, as I began to recognize this pattern, whenever I found myself attracted to someone, I would ask my gay colleague to check with the gay community before I initiated any contact. I was learning, however slowly, to protect myself from disappointment.

But, this was not leading me to the underlying reason I was bringing lesbians into my life. Feeling very frustrated, I had to ask why, given all the single women in my environment, I kept being attracted to gay women. Even with all the frustration I was experiencing, there was a silver lining. I was developing some remarkably beautiful and intimate opposite-sex friendships for the first time in my life. These were not just buddyships or colleagueships, and they didn't include all the expectations that often accompany romantic relationships.

What I found was that without the romantic attachment, all the role playing, and expectations that surround a typical romantic relationship, I was free to explore a much wider range of my emotions. I found I could be much more honest and open about myself when not worrying about a courtship. I also watched my lesbian friends have the same difficulties with romantic relationships as the heterosexual couples I knew. Each shared with me difficulties they were having with the other, and I began to feel honored to be a sounding board for each.

I was learning how to intimately relate to women on a non-romantic basis. Of even greater importance, I was getting in touch with my own feelings and needs. I was opening up to myself as much as I was to others. I was learning to have a relationship with myself, a major lesson for me.

I asked myself if it really were possible for a man and a woman to be so intimate, supportive, and caring for each other without being in a romantic relationship. It was a question I remembered from the movie "When Harry met Sally." I usually associated a strong love relationship with romantic love. Could one love another without romance as a main component? In my case, I had made it a little easier for myself, since even the potential for a romantic relationship was absent in these situations.

Looking back after several years, I realize how creative I was at that time without knowing it. Getting in touch with my emotions in a safe environment was just what I needed, and the way the situation unfolded was perfect for me, given the vulnerable, needy, and lonely state I was in. Otherwise, I would have probably immediately jumped into another relationship and most likely repeated my old patterns.

Eventually I had a non-physical relationship with a woman who loved baseball, both as player and fan. When I first met her she was in a co-dependent relationship with a high school teacher. She hated her parents, and was incapable of real intimacy. But I did love those baseball games we shared! She was the first woman I'd known who shared my enthusiasm for sports.

In the back of my mind, but only partially acknowledged, was the belief that I could help heal her problems, and then she would love me the way I wanted to be loved. I fantasized about how this relationship would evolve once she was healed. I was very attached to a romantic outcome for the two of us. I wanted her to show a great deal of physical affection toward me, and to share my interests. She knew she was closed up sexually and thought I could help her. Occasionally, she would sit in my lap, but very rigidly, like it was good medicine. I thought I had to be patient with her.

I couldn't understand her angry outbursts toward me. She accused me of being insensitive to her needs, yet I was trying to help her. I also wasn't accepting her as she was. I wanted to change her to become my partner in a fantasy. Was she picking up on my lack of acceptance, even though I saw my caretaking as being helpful and supportive. I became increasingly aware that my personality characteristic of wanting to take care of everyone wasn't very healthy, although it was some time before I did anything about it. I went to several twelve-step meetings at Co-Dependent Anonymous to show a willingness to learn, and to show support for her. This caretaking was not without condition. I did not give love freely and without expectation. Although I would not admit it, I expected she would eventually appreciate what I had done and show it through attention to me and my needs.

She kept telling me that she did not know how to behave in a relationship that wasn't co-dependent. With a good deal of patience and caretaking, I finally agreed with her that the relationship would be best if it ended. Although there was some sadness, I also felt a sense of relief when it did finally end.

A later relationship lasted for almost a year. It was by far the most satisfying one I experienced, particularly from the physical point of view. For years, I had been trying to manifest a very physical relationship, the lack of which was frustrating for me. This woman wanted a strong physical relationship. Given my history of attracting nonsexual friendships, this was a glorious opportunity to explore a rapidly expanding sensual side of myself. It was as beautiful as my fantasies. I learned a lot about allowing myself to experience the pleasure of being in a human body. Yet, something was still missing. Although our values were quite similar, our tastes and interests were not; our preferences in music and occupational interests were quite different. We did not have much in common to talk about or share.

We each had expectations for the other person to fulfill, particularly around shared interests and activities. Neither of us chose to be fully responsible for our dissatisfaction with the relationship, which each thought lay with the other person. We did become very good friends again after a couple of years, which was a wonderful lesson in itself about healing dissolved relationships.

This relationship was very important in showing me I could create a sensual relationship, but just one quality was not sufficient for a more complete partnership. I had to really find out what I wanted, and be clearer about my intent. Following this relationship, I put considerable time and effort into designing a relationship I thought would make me happy. But, I still had some healing to do.

The woman I was attracted to after I made my list for a desired relationship gave me one more opportunity to deal with my caretaking predisposition, and also with an issue of trusting the heart, versus the head. This woman had come from an abusive family, married an abuser, left that relationship, and then attracted another abusive man into her life. I may have represented her determination to make a change, since she had just left the second relationship. However, she had issues of control and manipulation that had not been healed which I felt she did not want to confront. I found when I was with her, I was very uncomfortable and feeling defensive most of the time. There was nothing obvious from what she said or did that explained why I felt this way. My intuition was picking something up my logical mind was missing (or resisting). There was a com-

munication going on beneath the words and actions exchanged. A wall existed between us.

My head kept telling me she had all the characteristics
I was looking for, while my heart kept sending out warnings taking the form of discomfort when I was around her.
I felt very judged in her presence, even though it was hard
to identify where this feeling was coming from.

Very slowly, I was beginning to see how all the available single women I was attracted to were my teachers and
healers. A pattern was beginning to emerge. Was I actually creating my ideal relationship a step at a time?

I asked McDermott why I was having so much difficulty
finding my ideal partner. He told me that the process of
creating this relationship and all the attendant learning
was a major path I chose for this lifetime. The real romantic relationship I was creating was with life itself; a romantic partner would simply reflect this back to me.

"The romantic aspect of your life is like a painting or artis-
tic creation, like a painter would create a masterpiece. So,
in a sense, it has all aspects of yourself intricately involved
in its energy field. You will be driven to create this great
masterpiece, and it comes from heart, soul and mind, and
not just from the mental itself. It is the most alive and organic form for you. The relationship is like an evolving can-
vas of a painting, ever moving forward. The colors and the
lines are always changing into a higher state. The relationship will be your great painting. Only you shall live it!"

After I heard this statement, I began to see all the previous frustrating individual relationships in a different
light. They were all part of a plan designed to achieve that
longed-for relationship. Why didn't I see it before? The gay
women served to help me develop intimate and self-dis-
closing friendships. Others helped me go beyond sexual

attraction alone, and realize a more peaceful, sensual side. Still others reflected back to me unhealthy issues around caretaking which I needed to correct.

Relationships took on a different meaning. I recognized how some of my relationships were mirroring parts of myself I could not accept, or needed to be healed. I looked for the meaning and learning the attraction would reveal. What qualities about myself was this person reflecting or bringing out in me? Was this meant to be a full blown romantic relationship that could emerge at some later point? I felt the friendship was the more important foundation to develop.

Ellen was a particularly important teacher of the principle of non-expectation. I found her immediately interesting and moderately attractive. She was slim and had a pleasant smile. What impressed me in particular was that she was a toucher; she spoke with her hands as well as with words.

On our first date, she snuggled up to me while we attended an outdoor concert of classical music; it was a wonderful experience. We both loved walks by the lake. She was very intelligent, open to new experiences, interested in cultural events, and loved gourmet dining; an interest I had not explored, but was ready to try. Through her enthusiasm I learned to appreciate eating exotic foods in foreign restaurants.

I also greatly admired her independence and self-sufficiency. I was amazed when she chose to have a candlelight dinner by herself, rather than to go with me to a concert. She inspired me to do more things on my own. Before, I would never have thought of attending plays or concerts without going with someone. Now, I not only do this as a challenge for myself, but actually enjoy the experience. There is a joy in being with oneself, as well as a joy in sharing with someone else.

Although independent, and sometimes intense, she was not aloof and distant. She had a willingness to grow and learn, and we never lacked for conversation. Once, when she had a particularly bad day, she called me to be with her, not to talk about it, but to hold her, and stroke her hair. Another time, I had a particularly disappointing experience, and we went out to an interesting restaurant, and she listened while I got the frustration off my chest. I felt so much better by the end of the evening. We hugged each other. We relaxed and healed in different ways suiting our individual temperaments, but we could be there for each other openly and honestly.

We didn't have a lot of dates. Sometimes weeks would go by without seeing or talking with each other. Then we might see each other several times within a short span. I was never sure where our relationship was going, and at times I experienced some frustration. It wasn't romantic, but it seemed more than just friendship. Intellectually, she was very challenging, and we did have some heated discussions, although they tended to diminish over time. Usually, I was able to return to the appreciation of the moment, and to be okay with the indeterminacy of the relationship.

I saw her over a period of about six months. Just before we met, she had broken up with someone she cared deeply about. She was not ready for a new relationship. She was concerned with finding a new job, and was unable to do so in the Burlington area. Opportunities in other areas of the country drew her away. Knowing her was a wonderful experience, and I have not regretted the time we shared together.

About two months after Ellen left town, Claire came into my life. I met Claire in Florida, at a continuing care residency for older people where my widowed mother was living. I was amazed to meet someone of my age at this facility. The small talk soon turned to more personal and spiritual topics. Both of us experienced what can only be described as a communication limitation due to the fact we couldn't talk fast enough. Multiple thoughts would arise into our consciousness simultaneously, and we had to deliberately slow down and choose which ideas we wanted to express verbally. Such a means of communication seemed very inadequate. We acted like we were old friends who hadn't seen each other in years and were now trying to catch up all at once. We found ourselves very much in agreement about what we were sharing. Not only had we both spent time in Burlington, but we also grew up in the same small town in New Jersey. It was obvious to both of us that this was no accidental meeting.

In Claire I have found someone who not only shares my interests and values, but also brings a wonderful sense of openness, acceptance and playfulness to our relationship. With her I feel more alive than ever. She seems to bring out more of me. Her honesty and sincerity allow me to trust and accept myself even more. We can talk for hours about anything, feeling totally vulnerable in each other's presence. I admire her independence and vibrancy, even though she is almost totally blind.

However, there are some interesting logistical obstacles to the growth of this relationship. First, she lives four hours away. We do talk regularly on the phone, and I have visited her. She is going through a difficult divorce, and is experiencing the difficulties of being a single mother. She cannot leave the state she is in without relinquishing custody of her daughter. Her income is derived from her out-of-home work as a massage therapist, and it has taken her a while to build up a dependable clientele.

A few months ago, I might have either totally disregarded her because of all these restraints, or gone headlong into an intense effort to make it work according to a romantic scenario. Romance may still be a possibility, even though it seems remote at the moment. But, I am at peace with other outcomes as well, including a wonderful friendship. So, at present, I have not attained the ideal relationship I have been seeking for almost a decade. However, I am more allowing. And I have become much more comfortable with the process itself. I have a sense of peace, lightness, and gentle anticipation that didn't exist earlier when I was much more needy and impatient. I am living more in the present, and appreciating more and more what unfolds from moment to moment. I am becoming aware that each relationship takes me a step closer to the desired romantic partnership: first, with myself as I allow for greater wholeness; and, second, with a woman who will reflect my new relationship with myself. The creation is unfolding a step at a time.

———————

Since the breakup of his marriage, Mark has come a long way in accepting and enjoying the relationships that have emerged in his life. One major result is that he has been learning to appreciate learning. He has realized that all of his past relationships have value in themselves. His decision to create a new relationship after the trauma of his divorce set in motion a whole series of learning opportunities which enabled him to grow in intimacy and love, not only towards others, but particularly toward himself. He was in a very needy state when he started, but over time he learned that the experiences coming his way were not the result of bad luck, but were all part of the process of obtaining his goals.

When he was first divorced, he had no idea who he was, or what he valued in a relationship. Initially, he needed to develop a strong relationship with himself...a sense of wholeness, according to McDermott. Mark had to be solid and self-sufficient with himself in order to move past the states of neediness and incompleteness; a desire to caretake and control. Mark's open choice to create a new romantic relationship to replace his first marriage, set in motion the manifestation of experiences, including confusing and uncomfortable relationships, which his conscious self could not understand or analyze.

In desiring such a dream relationship, Mark opened a closet of fear and pain which blocked the thing he most yearned for. He needed to clean out this emotional closet in order for the manifestation of his dream to materialize. First, he had to identify what he wanted. Next, he had to learn to trust the creative process which he had set in motion to achieve the desire. He eventually realized that all of the relationships he was attracting to himself were assisting him to attain his goal; a wonderful partnership.

Second, because of the process involved, Mark has learned to enjoy being in the moment. Surrendering to the present did not mean he relinquished the intent to achieve the relationship he desired. He found there is supreme trust, enjoyment, and absorption in the moment. According to Sir Garrod, it is possible to be intensely curious without judgment about, or need to measure progress toward, a potential outcome. An individual simply cannot see all of the pieces as they form the path leading toward the desired goal.

Susan's Story

One member of our group, Susan, went through two major relationships that did not work out, but both served to prepare her for the relationship she sought. The last relationship she attracted just before meeting her future husband was very helpful for her learning process. Susan's experiences helped us to see how all of the relationships during our past that didn't succeed were actually bringing up important issues which needed to be faced and dealt with. Her history helped us look at past situations from a different perspective, enabling us to find the beautiful patterns of healings and lessons they contained which led toward desired goals.

Susan had attracted a multimillionaire. He expected her to be his personal servant; someone to wait on him. She knew the universe put her in this position as an opportunity to heal a long standing perception she had of herself. In the past she would have given up everything for him. The lure of financial support he could give her was a powerful incentive. She was cleaning homes for a living, and the thought of having enough money so she wouldn't have to do such hard work was tempting.

Susan told us that she saw this relationship as a "great test I manifested for myself. You are attracting someone with a personal flaw to help you meet your own challenges. What I had to learn was to rely on myself for my own happiness. Every relationship I have gotten into has been there for my growth. It will happen when it is right. With this last relationship, I feel I have gotten to the place where I can be alone, and earn enough to support myself for the rest of my life. If I don't have real love, I don't want a relationship."

She accepted the personal flaws of her previous infatuations as education to prepare her for what she really wanted. She chose to heal her beliefs around her role in a relationship, recognize her ability to provide for herself, and clearly define what it was she wanted. Finally, she chose to believe in her own worthiness to receive. As our attitudes become healthier, our relationships will mirror that healing.

Joan's Story

Joan had just about given up ever finding a partner. Two previous marriages had failed, and subsequent relationships were also major disappointments. Joan was a regular member of our manifestation group when she manifested her ideal partner. Whereas Susan had a clear sense of what she wanted in terms of personality characteristics, love, and respect, Joan had very specific interests she wanted to manifest in her partner.

————◆◆◆◆◆————

Although I yearned for a compatible someone I could share my life with, I had just about decided with [the end of] my most recent relationship that all the good men were taken, and since I really felt quite whole by myself, I would, regrettably, stop looking.

Soon after I made this decision, I was attending the monthly meeting of dowsers where the topic was on crystals. I sat in the front row facing a large table of beautiful rocks that actually seemed to exert a force over me. I felt charged, vibratory, charmed, light headed, and pleasantly woozy by the end of the class. This was interesting since I had little interest in crystals, actually shunning reading about them, prejudging their fare to be faddish.

I approached the speaker, who was also selling them, to buy a beautiful red one. She said in a southern drawl, "Honey, you don't need red. You are red; but you do need a pink. How about a rose quartz? And, by the way, how is your love life?"

"Terrible," I said, "and I don't like pink."

"That's why it is terrible," she said. "Choose a rose quartz and hold it while you meditate on the ideal mate for you. But, be sure of what you ask for, because that's what you'll get."

"How silly," I thought, when back home, as I sat down to meditate, "but I ought to give it a go—just for a lark."

At this stage of my life, I pretty much knew by experience the attributes I wanted in a man (such as high character, gentle, loving, inner strength and sensitivity), but I also wanted compatible likes which I hadn't had before, so I went wild. I wanted someone who liked to dance, specifically folk and contra dance; someone who loved music, specifically classical music; someone who has not only a good brain, but a good mind, specifically a physicist with an imagination; someone who likes nature and the out of doors, specifically someone who likes to hike and cross country ski and canoe; and, while I'm at it, someone with a handsome face, healthy body and about 6 foot 2. The height I threw in for a joke, almost to tempt the fates to see what they'd do with it.

Time passed. Five weeks to be exact. I had forgotten about this, when a past companion informed me he had met a man whom he thought I would have a lot in common with, and who wished to meet me if I was interested. Dubiously, I said yes, I'll try one more. The one more that I met a few weeks later turned out to be my most wonderful mani-festation. My husband Johann teaches college physics, plays viola, is a professional singer and a conductor of the choral society I now sing in. He loves folk dancing, and we dance often. He is an inveterate hiker, summer and winter camper, canoes, cross country skis, loves the out of doors, is a gentle, friendly, handsome person with a beautiful soul and body, strong and healthy, and, you guessed it, and I asked for it and I got it — he is six foot two!

Learning to Trust More Easily

Sir Garrod pointed out the relationship Joan desired came after a long period of manifesting undesirable rela-tionships. And, even though she may have experienced dis-couragement after each relationship, she was growing and learning, and becoming clearer and more certain about what she really wanted in a life partner. She had set in motion a path that would eventually bring the desired relationship to her.

One of the last steps was to let go, and, in a sense, give up. With the crystals, she pretended, and treated the expe-rience more like a game. She was not attached to the out-come, nor did she act out of desperation or need. First, she gave up looking, although her preference was still to create a partner. Then, after she meditated on her crystal, she forgot about it.

Sir Garrod noted that when a goal is stated in terms that allow the highest and best to develop, "it breaks the cycle within the person's mind which says, 'I must work very hard to make this happen. If it doesn't happen, I will be a failure. And, if it does happen, I will be a miracle worker.' All of this is ego involvement. When we allow the universe to provide the best and highest resolution, we completely eliminate the ego function, and then the energy pattern can work directly."

We were told that anytime we had a strong desire or attachment to a specific goal, and felt that only by achieving this goal we would be complete or worthy, we were showing a lack of love for ourselves. This lack of love prevents our goals from manifesting.

Sir Garrod explains, "If you tell the universe you want a desired goal, then you must surrender to the universe and let it go to work for you. An archer desires to hit a target; then for the arrow to hit the target one must let the arrow go, or it will not fly. If you constantly pick at it, and worry about it, you will continually disturb it, and the universe will not be able to help you. It is done through the energy of the universe. When you plant a seed, you do not pick at the seed to see if it is growing. It is the energy of the universe that creates the flower."

It struck us that Joan had simply allowed the process to unfold, although she was often not aware of how it was happening. She created a dream, leaving it up to the universe to bring contact from a friend to discover the relationship. There was no doubt she had created the relationship; her energy field had brought it to her. As humans, we cannot see into our future, and it is difficult for us to understand how it all fits together. All we can do is trust, and know we deserve what our heart truly desires. E v e r y - thing we could want exists, and the manifestation process simply sets up cooperative energy flows to bring the elements (or, partners in this case) together. There is no scarcity of wonderful partners.

So many relationships which to us, at first, appeared to be negative, were actually part of the learning experience that created our desired outcome. Trust, and your higher self will bring the right partner to you at the right time.

Tim's Story

Trusting, and not being needy or attached to a relationship, were big issues for me before I was able to attract my wife. When I was in my twenties and thirties, I kept having relationships that weren't working for me. Most of my friends were married, and the marriage of my best friend reminded me all the more of my unwanted single state.

It wasn't that I couldn't attract women, but rather that I couldn't attract the right woman. I was very attached to needing to have a partner. I wasn't aware of how this attachment sets up an energy of neediness which actually pushed people away. I was always looking, and quite lonely while I was looking. The right person was scared off by my neediness, and those needy women who found me attractive, I didn't want. I had two trial marriages which did not work out. It was clear to me that what I was doing was not resulting in a satisfactory relationship.

A friend encouraged me to get therapy, which helped me see that my problems were not all that unique. Before this, I thought I was all alone with this frustration. Now I could learn through other people's experiences.

I continued to be anxious to have a relationship, but made an effort to do all the right things; to clean up my act, so to speak. For example, I no longer used a checklist for each woman I met to see how well she stacked up against a list of ideals I had formulated. When, even after doing all the right things, nothing was happening, I went to the group leader and asked him when I would meet her. He responded, "When you are ready," which only made me more frustrated. It would have been more helpful, I thought, if he had told me where to move, or locate, or what strategy I might use to attract her. I was still looking for an external answer, instead of realizing it was my internal readiness that would bring her to me.

Some healing must have been put into motion at a subconscious level, because a few weeks later in the middle of a conversation with a friend at work, a wonderful feeling unexpectedly came over me. I suddenly let it go. It was like a huge burden was lifted off my shoulders. I remembered saying "wow" to my friend, and then skipping down the hall—something you never did at work.

At some point I had crossed the boundary, and was able to let it be. I was no longer attached to an outcome. It didn't matter whether I ever found her or not. Of course, it was about a week later that I met my present wife at a ski function. Although I didn't know it at the time, since she had no ring on, she was a married woman. I was attracted to her and felt good chemistry between us.

When she told me she was married, I was not at all angry or disappointed. A few years earlier, my reaction would have been quite different. Then, I was only concerned with finding a wife and would have crossed her off. Instead I suggested we be friends, and since we belonged to the same ski club, we continued to meet at scheduled club times. I felt there was an abundance of women around and would have no trouble finding a relationship, so I could enjoy our friendship too.

What I didn't know at that time was that her marriage had been in trouble, and three months later she left her husband and soon after that we began dating. I was glad I didn't know about the trouble in her relationship until after the separation had occurred.

The key for me was giving up the attachment—the need for a relationship. I had tried to do all the right things, and none helped. It was only when I finally gave up, that the relationship I desired materialized. That releasing seemed to create an opening; a readiness that hadn't existed before.

It still seems strange to me, even having worked with this concept for some time now, that it is when we truly "give up" and accept whatever manifests, that the desired relationship, object, or experience appears.

Bill's Story

We will conclude this chapter with the case history of a married couple where a suspected affair threatens to break up the marriage. Certainly this situation poses the greatest challenge for forgiveness and understanding.

Bill became suspicious when a close friend told him he had seen Bill's wife in a bar. She was acting very friendly with another man, a business acquaintance. His friend couldn't tell the depth of feelings being shown, but his warning did alert Bill's suspicions. His wife had been working late more and more frequently. He originally thought the overtime was attributed to the seasonal requirements of her job. Now he wasn't so sure. She also seemed much more distant, more careful around him. Was she acting guilty?

———

"My suspicions continued to grow. Things I had not even noticed a few days earlier now took on new significance. I began to see infidelity all around me. She was too tired to go to the office party. Before, even when she was at her busiest, she almost never had to go into work on the weekend. That was sacred time for us. Now, she was working weekends.

I thought about confronting her with the truth and demanding she give him up. But suppose she didn't? I wanted to preserve this relationship. Even if I made her give him up, what would stop her from going back to him, or finding someone else in the future? I might get her to leave him, perhaps through catalyzing feelings of guilt, but even if that was successful, what would that buy me in the long run?

It was very difficult for me to accept the fact that I was helpless to change things. Sadness swept over me like clouds of gloom. I was becoming resigned that what I feared the most might become a reality."

———•·•·•———

Bill contemplated several scenarios of ways he could change the course of his relationship: 1) he could find a relationship of his own...that would get even with her; 2) he could suggest they both see a marriage counselor...but, she would never do that; 3) he could threaten to leave her first...unless she was thoroughly sure about her relationship, she would have to realize how vulnerable she was; or, 4) He could let her leave, and play on the sympathy of the court. It was reasonable to assume that in any settlement, sympathy would be weighed in his favor. This put him in a good position to be awarded custody, or at least control, of the children. The thought of losing her children would terrify her.

Bill went through all these scenarios and could see, in the long run, none really served to give him what he wanted. At best, any were short-term fixes. He might be able to force his wife to stay in the relationship, but he knew he could not force her to love him. Any ultimatum would only put distance between them. He wanted a relationship that worked; not one that appeared to on the surface. He realized he could not control the outcome. Although self-interest was his motivation, it was at this point he *let go* and allowed the universe to solve his problem.

———◦◦◦———

Thoughts about former relationships prior to my marriage, and how they ended, passed through my mind. It became clear to me that I wanted to part friends, as I had wanted to in earlier relationships, and resolve the issues between us as best we could. I realized that I wanted a committed monogamous relationship, but how it would play out, and with whom, I decided to give up to my higher self to take care of.

I recognized I had a choice as to how I reacted to my wife's behavior. I had to examine my motives for my choice of reaction. I chose to give up my desire for a specific outcome regarding my wife. I asked my higher self to create the appropriate scenario for my own and my wife's highest good. If this meant parting, I would accept that outcome.

The way I reclaimed my power was to give it up and change how I perceived the situation. I made it okay for her to do what she was doing. I faced the fear to the end and lived through it. When I examined the worst scenario— separation, I could see I would survive. I let it go and said, "The hell with it. I allow her to be who she is. I accept whatever is to follow. I accept her. I love her!"

Relief washed over me. Within moments I sensed a shift in our energies. That same day, my wife began crying and started talking to me. She, too, said she noticed the shift in energy; like a wall had shattered that was between us. Suddenly, it seemed like energy was flowing from her to me and back again. The lines of communication were open.

———◦◦◦———

Bill learned his wife had not been having an affair, although she did admit she was attracted to her colleague. She had been undergoing enormous stress at work and felt she couldn't burden Bill with her problems, because of the stress he had been confronting in his own life. They talked and cried for many hours after that. The healing of their marriage had begun.

At the moment Bill gave up any desire to manipulate the results, chose to accept his wife as she was, and allowed his higher self to direct the outcome, the impasse dissolved and they were able to reconcile. Each time he consulted his higher self, he knew his one real choice was to trust, even if this meant facing his fear of losing his wife. He had to brave the possibility of divorce, and trust that if that was the consequence, however undesirable it seemed, then that would be all right, too. He realized he couldn't figure it out on a conscious level. Letting go opened up the opportunity for change.

When it became all right for the relationship to take whatever course it needed to, that impasse was breached. It was not that he wasn't clear in his desire for a renewed relationship with his wife, but that he trusted his higher self to bring to him what was in his, and her, best interest. Once again, the interesting paradox that we tend to get what we want when we relinquish control and give up having to have it, is illustrated.

Conclusion

Where responsibility to self, detachment from outcome, and appreciation of the unique gifts and talents of each other are present, a healthy, loving partnership follows. Many of our relationship problems result from trying to control the other partner, which can rarely be done successfully. Often, we want the other person to change to meet our needs. The more we meet our own needs, the less we have to rely on someone else to do so.

In manifesting a romantic relationship, it is ironic that when we let go and surrender our desired goal to the universe (in a sense, give up), we are the most successful in obtaining that which we desire. It is often impossible to anticipate the best process to achieve our goal. Surrendering the process to the universe and allowing manifestations of the third kind to present themselves, is often the easiest and most effortless solution. In Mark's case, a series of relationships helped him heal parts of himself, which would then allow a much healthier relationship to materialize. Following a series of relationships, Joan was successful by forming a detailed manifestation request employing a crystal.

Just as the body may pass through many treatments and learning opportunities during healing, it is possible to experience a number of relationships which present growth opportunities designed to heal the self, and are part of the path to obtain a desired relationship. Learning to trust and accept the higher self, allowing the relationships to present lessons and not judging the outcomes (particularly viewing broken relationships as failures), were important lessons for many of those who shared their stories.

McDermott tried to explain to us, using an analogy based on computers, about the complexity involved in how our conscious manifestations are only a part of other requests and decisions we have made beyond our consciousness. In turn, all of these desires of our own are cooperatively matched with the desires of others to maximize the growth opportunities of all involved.

How, McDermott asks, can we, with our limited, focused, consciousness, possibly determine all of the outcomes, much less the paths leading to those outcomes? Although we always have a choice, surrendering the process to the universe is often the simplest and most effortless way to realize a desired goal.

McDermott says, "Imagine you are all still souls and have not, as yet, manifested on the physical plane. Before you have chosen your parents and the growth process, and the opportunities for the growth process of this life, you go to heavenly planning meetings. At these meetings are a great number of souls also planning their incarnations. And, if you want to use computers, we would say there are some powerful spiritual entities who listen to your requests, and put them into the computer with the others. Then you get to see what possibilities exist on the physical plane for these patterns of growth. As many experiential possibilities as possible are matched up. Once this is done, there is agreement on the parts of all the individuals. So, when you come into the physical form you have actually put into motion the energy to create the experiences and the opportunities of your physical life based on choices from a high level of awareness. If you choose the highest and best path for you with each opportunity, you will eventually align with all of these others that are appropriate for your growth and their own."

If we can trust what McDermott says, that we create all of our relationships, and that many of them have been set in motion even before we incarnate, then the question to be raised concerns the reasons we have so much difficulty judging the relationships we attract into our lives. Why did Mary panic when her lover chose someone else? Why did Mark experience so much frustration when the women he attracted were gay, or co-dependent, or unhappy with him?

Our fears keep us from accepting the people who come into our lives to work with us on our lessons; fears that often center around self worth. These ego-based fears tell our conscious minds, "Without a partner I will be lonely, and others will see me as a failure. My needs will go unmet without a spouse. If I don't attract someone, or, don't keep someone from straying, then there is something wrong with me."

Bill had to examine all of the possible outcomes he feared before he could let go and accept his wife as she was. After he had explored all of the paths of potential control and manipulation available to him, and the fears associated with each, only unconditional love brought the resolution he desired. The interesting thing is, when Bill recognized and embraced his fears, then surrendered and let go, he freed both himself and his wife.

Chapter 7

Facing Death

An earlier chapter explored the difficulties of trusting our own inner guidance to suggest a healing path for a chronic illness, especially when it is in direct conflict with medical authority. The last chapter on relationships cited people challenged to trust their inner guidance and accept the relationships, and the conflicts, they had created as part of their path toward learning and growth.

The real test of listening for inner guidance and practicing acceptance comes when we face death. For many of us, facing our own mortality because of a life-threatening disease is one of the most frightening experiences we can have while in human form. Sir Garrod tells us, our focused conscious self simply cannot "see" from the expanded perception of the higher self the insignificance of the transition between the physical and spiritual state. We have been born and we have died countless times during an infinite number of incarnations, but our conscious self is able to experience only the present incarnation.

Nor, according to Sir Garrod, can the limited human consciousness comprehend all the meaningful connections and lessons between its present self and all of its other incarnations. It certainly cannot comprehend the lessons of all other human entities with whom it interacts, and who have consented to cooperate in joint learning experiences. For example, a spirit does not simply choose a set of parents for its learning; the parents choose that entity, as well. During other lifetimes, the roles may have been reversed (parent and child; male and female; antagonist and protagonist, etc.). Not only do all humans have their own individual lessons, but entire groups may be simultaneously working on group lessons. Entire families, or nations, may unite for mutual learning purposes.

Death is simply "no big deal" from the higher self's perspective. Time and space, at least as we know it, does not exist in the spiritual state. Countless individuals are constantly passing back and forth between the spirit and physical states. On the spirit level, death is merely a transition from one state of existence to another, no more upsetting than changing jobs.

However, the conscious self does not view the big picture, and a life-threatening disease can create a reaction of great anxiety and fear, and precipitate a feverish search for a cure. Since, from the higher self's perspective, death is an illusion, the need to find a cure may not be that important. Real learning takes place during the process. But, as humans, this is still difficult to comprehend.

Jeff's diagnosis of cancer elicited a reaction of fear and anxiety. Although, over time, a spiritual perspective provided some comfort, the ego's investment in survival was paramount during much of Jeff's course. As he waited at the doctor's office for the results of his surgery, he reflected on the power of the illusion of physical reality. Never in his life was he required to confront such a range of emotion as he encountered during the preceding two months.

Jeff's Story

The waiting room was crowded. It was going to be a long

time until my turn to meet with Dr. Boswell, the surgeon who only five days before removed one of my lymph nodes to test for the spread of the cancer. Now I would receive the results of the tests. To say I was nervous about the outcome, was to greatly understate my feelings of apprehension.

If the outcome was negative, would I have let all my friends down who had prayed so diligently for my recovery? How would I tell my sons at the tender age of eighteen, for whom death was a very distant mystery when their whole lives lay in front of them. And, what would I say to my eighty-seven year old mother, who didn't even know I had a melanoma in the first place.

Most of all, I was afraid of what this told me about my own lack of power to create good health. After all, I had been working diligently on my spiritual growth. Was this an indication of my own failure to follow a correct spiritual path? I didn't want to die, and I didn't understand why I was even afraid of death. From my fairly extensive reading, I knew that death was merely a transition to a more expanded and joyous state of consciousness. It meant returning to our natural home, our true state of existence. I had read hundreds of accounts of near-death experiences, and absorbed so much New Age material on the persistence of the soul and eternal, life that I was bewildered by my ongoing fear of death itself. Even with all the many hours [I spent] with Sir Garrod and McDermott since the original diagnosis of my cancerous lesion, when it came right down to the final prognosis, I was still fearful.

The doctor stuck his head into the waiting room, acknowledged my presence, apologized for the wait, and offered me a cup of coffee. I knew then it was going to be a long wait. Many of the same people were still there from when I first arrived.

My mind drifted back to that first rainy November afternoon when Dr. Rosetti, my dermatologist, her assistant, and her colleague all told me that I should have the dark, multi-colored, brown lesion located just under my left shoulder removed as soon as possible. It was likely cancer, but a biopsy would first have to go to the lab for analysis. It hit me. The big "C" word. My whole world suddenly seemed to be collapsing around me, so great was my fear.

I needed a few minutes of time by myself, away from the white coated experts urging me to take immediate action. Photos of huge, ugly melanomas, blown up ten or twenty times, stared down at me from the walls, frightening me even more. The doctors' projected fear for my condition, along with giving me little reassurance, made the situation seem far graver than it actually was. Doctors seemed to like to paint worst case scenarios. Perhaps this was to impress upon you the seriousness of the matter, so a patient will take action. But it also has the effect of creating so much fear that I wanted to run as fast, and as far away as I could, and deny the feeling of helplessness. To me, the fact they were going to perform the biopsy that same afternoon was a scary message in itself about how serious they thought my cancer was.

A tremendous feeling of anxiety and panic set in. In a matter of a few minutes, my future was doubtful. I didn't know whether I would be able to go to the office on Monday, or if I'd see my children graduate from college.

I phoned my friend David, poured out my fear, and worked through many of my doubts during our conversation, at least to the point of knowing what action to take. David was very supportive, always guiding me to come up with my own answers, rather than telling me what to do, or even what he himself would do under similar circumstances.

When I returned to the doctor's office for outpatient surgery half an hour later, I was surprisingly calm and much more accepting. I even noted that David happened to be near the phone that day to offer his support, and that my son, who almost never can be found during afternoons, had unexpectedly stopped by my office and was willing to drive me home after the surgery. There was a flow to what was going on. It was even Friday, thus, I probably wouldn't have any disruption to my work schedule. Once I had accepted the situation, there was something appealing about being able to take quick action. A person's greatest fear comes from a state of feeling helpless. Boy, did I find that out!

Although the intern was very somber and businesslike, the nurse was very sympathetic to New Age literature and the concept of a mind/body connection. She was familiar with some of the alternative healing methods I was interested in, and we had a lively discussion while I was being prepared for surgery. I remembered being asked what kind of music I liked as they pointed to a radio sitting on a chair in the corner. At that point, I was too engaged in conversation to really want music. Also, I was loving the energy of the surgeon. She was intelligent, caring, gentle, and had a nice sense of humor. This was in contrast to when I first met her; then she was very distant and businesslike, even frightening with the diagnosis.

Now she was talking with me and the attending nurse. She, too, believed there was something to this mind/body concept, and suggested I use both traditional and New Age methods to cure my cancer.

My attention returned to the present. Two more patients checked in. Not too long now, I thought, as I looked around the waiting room. I found my thoughts returning to the last time I had experienced this much fear. It was four days after the biopsy when the diagnosis of cancer was confirmed. It was two o'clock on a Tuesday afternoon. The nurse who assisted Dr. Rosetti with the surgery told me the results. I will never forget the paralyzing and all-consuming fear I was left with.

David and I spent the better part of the following day exploring the origins and consequences of my fears; fears centered around loss of control, images of being incapacitated, hair falling out, and becoming dependent on others. We made a list of the fears—it helped to objectify them. Being alone, imposing on friends, wondering how to tell relatives, and losing faith in oneself, emerged as the greatest fears. All that I presently enjoyed, music, spiritual growth, and friendships would now be dominated by this condition; a pervading cloud overshadowing everything I previously enjoyed. How could I enjoy anything with a death sentence always hanging in the background. It didn't matter that I knew we all die someday, many instantly (such as in car accidents), while others die in the prime of their lives. It didn't matter. It was <u>my</u> personal life on the line. How primal the fear around survival.

What did help, was David reminding me of some of the positive features about death. The mysteries around the meaning of life that intrigued me would now be much more accessible. Secrets of the other side that taunt me would be revealed in all of their magnificence.

Even though my explorations on what life was like after death were done on an intellectual level, they still offered me considerable comfort. The radiant embrace of unconditional love and joy was something to look forward to. People who went through near death experiences described situations of inexplicable bliss, and when they returned to physical existence all fear of death was lost.

David and I began to consider how much fun it might be to come back as a channeled entity, maybe even using David as the medium. Would I be able to tell him what lottery number to play? Perhaps I could tell him which golf course would have the best playing conditions on a particular day. Even more importantly, I could use David to relay information from the other side, like Sir Garrod was doing for us in the present. It seemed our friendship would add a degree of authenticity and intimacy to channeling which is not presently available.

In the spiritual state I wouldn't have to worry about time or health or mobility. Without a body I wouldn't have to worry about earning a living or paying taxes. I would be free from the cumbersomeness of a physical body and able to translocate from place to place in an instant. Without a body there would be no disease...and, no more cancer.

Of course, Sir Garrod had some very inspiring and comforting things to say to me when we had a channeling session a few days later. He kept stressing that the cancer should not be judged as an evil invader of the flesh, but rather as a messenger of healing and learning. The flesh was merely reflecting a lesson in the physical with origins on the spiritual plane. Evidently, trapped energy in my being wished to be released so that more joy could come into my life. I remember telling him it was a strange way of looking at cancer. "It doesn't feel like a gift to me," I said.

A major understanding of the spiritual source of the cancer came one evening when Sir Garrod referred to a past lifetime. I remembered how I felt when he first told me not to judge the condition like I did in my priest lifetime, but to let it be my teacher. "Priest Lifetime?" I asked. For a moment, I looked at Sir Garrod, wondering what he was referring to about my being a priest, and, even weirder, what this had to do with my skin cancer.

Of course I knew we are all multi-dimensional beings, with many interconnected selves from other lives which constantly influenced each other. I envisioned their inter-action to be like a huge organic dance of many energies, constantly exchanging information around a myriad of les-sons which are well beyond the comprehension of my lim-ited consciousness.

I learned from Sir Garrod that my cancer, at least in part, was related to a healing of the self esteem of another facet of myself that existed in another lifetime. It was like dealing with a repressed childhood trauma which now had to be recognized, experienced, and then healed. Only, in this case, I was dealing with another lifetime of mine, per-haps as much a part of me on a broader soul level as my present childhood experiences were still a part of and in-fluencing my life. If my "self" is actually much larger than what I experienced in this lifetime, then it must be true that at some level, conscious or unconscious, I am a prod-uct of those earlier experiences as well. As a result, self-judgments I made during a lifetime as a priest were still effecting me centuries later.

It seemed that 250 years ago in Ireland, I was a very unhappy priest. I was quite egotistical, and, according to Sir Garrod, made the mistake of striving for perfection. I thought I could live a life completely free of sin or mistakes if I devoted myself totally to the monastic life and rejected as much as I could of an earthly or physical existence.

Things moved very slowly in Dr. Boswell's office. I learned a long time ago never to go to a doctor's office with-out reading material, so I pulled out my notes and reread Sir Garrod's statements about the priest's life. He said,

"This was your ego dominating your consciousness. The larger part of yourself knew the foolishness of it. And the only way to get the Priest's attention in that life was to create a mistake, a fall from grace by making you betray your vows. The larger part of yourself was having a wonderful time, and laughing uproariously at the pompousness of your ego." How nice I provided entertainment for my higher self.

I had a hard time believing my higher self was an extension of me. It felt more like something imposed on me. I would never have chosen to suffer through having surgery and all the fears it brought up. If my higher self was me, why didn't I feel better than I did? Why was I so fearful and anxious? I knew it was because I was disconnected from that expanded part of my consciousness. I looked at my limited ego-consciousness and human body as the major source of my identity. Even though I intellectually recognized myself as a multidimensional being, the illusion of my humanness and separateness from my higher self, was more convincing to me as I contemplated my mortality.

I continued to read about the priest incarnation. "There was what you perceived to be a great weakness, a breaking down of the flesh—in plain language, having sex with someone you perceived to be beneath you. You had no respect for this woman, even though she tried to love you and to show you the truth of love. You could not allow it into your consciousness. You thought of her as evil, and as dirty as your own body. You judged this breakdown of the flesh as being a weakness and experienced enormous remorse and guilt for having been involved in this sinful and dirty act.

You had decided, through borrowing the church's perception of life, that a more holy experience exists with God than with another human being, which, of course, is to deny that this other human being is also God. Is it correct that you can have a greater relationship to God through celibacy, than through a relationship? Not from our perspective. The pathway to God is through every pathway that exists. There is no one pathway."

So, because of a Priest's perceived fall from grace 250 years ago, I have to undergo two operations for cancer. How could this be me? I remember just a few days ago, while spending two and a half hours in the operating room having my back and arm pit sliced open, wishing that Seventeenth Century Priest had gotten his act together and spared us both a lot of discomfort.

I had trouble understanding how there could be wonderful learning from this experience. According to Sir Garrod, the "gift" of cancer allowed me to bring all of my healing talents to bear on one major illness. As Sir Garrod said, this was like a great "wedding" where all the years of preparation were coming to a grand conclusion. I found it difficult to think of healing cancer as a wedding celebration.

Sir Garrod suggested I allow myself to be drawn to the healing methods appropriate for me. I needed to experience and embrace the emotions of fear, remorse, and guilt of this previous lifetime, and to forgive myself for my act of self-judgment. It was quite strange forgiving oneself for an act committed during another lifetime. Sometimes, it was unclear where the sadness was coming from, whether from this lifetime, the previous lifetime, or the present fear about cancer. But, I learned to let the emotions, whatever their source, to arise and flow through me.

One of the strangest experiences I had was being drawn to watch the eight-hour video version of the *The Thorn Birds* by Colleen McCullough. I read the book from cover to cover, but was even more moved by the movie version. I watched

it many times, experiencing enormous emotional sadness
during parts of the film centered around the romantic feelings of a woman for a priest who, although they had a brief
affair, chose power and status over love. By the end of the
film he recognized he had made the wrong choice, and experienced enormous remorse, guilt, and regret. I always
experience great waves of sadness, often crying, when wit-
nessing this scene.

I had been moved by this story many years before the
film came out, although I had no idea why. I strongly iden-
tified with the Priest, and got swept up in the emotions
again and again each time I watched it. It was powerfully
therapeutic, a catharsis. I was particularly drawn to the
scene where his inhibitions break down and he follows the
passion of his heart, if only for a brief time. Once again, he
agonized whether he really loves God more than he loves
the woman, as if it is the only real choice open to him.

My identification with the story of *The Thorn Birds* was
only one of many tools my inner self brought to heal the
part of my soul of which the cancer was just the outer expression—the impetus for me to do the necessary learning
and healing.

I visualized my cancer cells being attacked and killed
by healthy cells. At night, I fell asleep listening to a tape
especially designed for people with cancer which affirmed
health and creativity. I changed my diet slightly, feeling
the nourishment would not only defeat the cancer, but create a healthy body; my number one desire.

Sir Garrod encouraged me to use flower essences to work
on my energy field, release trapped emotions, and create
alignment and balance. Moreover, the act of choosing those
best for me using a dowsing technique would teach me to
learn to trust my internal guidance more.

I had wonderful support during this period. Learning to accept such support was a lesson in itself. I could feel the prayers and compassion of my friends, and they were always there when I needed them. It turned out that one very loving, supportive, individual was an intern, and she was in the operating room to talk to me during surgery. David and his wife were present after the surgery. I was never alone, except when I wanted to be.

I was amazed by the fascinating people I met during the entire medical process. Most people were very friendly. The person who drew my blood for a test knew of Sir Garrod, and was interested in talking about near death experiences. The anesthesiologist, whom I was supposed to meet with for a twenty minute pre-operation session, talked with me for an hour and a half about mind/body connections, and troubling issues he faced with people whose pain seemed psychosomatically induced, but would not accept that interpretation.

Even the head surgeon, Dr. Boswell, was a practitioner of transcendental meditation, although he seemed embarrassed to talk about it when I brought it up...particularly in the presence of others. In order to make friendly conversation during the operation, I asked him about his TM practice. At that point, he was about to make the incision in my armpit to get at the lymph node. I laughingly said I hoped he had done his meditation that day. One of the interns looked quizzically at him and asked, "Do you practice that stuff?" He gave a nervous laugh and said, "Sure." I didn't bring it up again. I sensed some embarrassment, and I didn't want to distract him from the task at hand. There may have been a conspiracy of silence among some of those in the medical profession, but there was also an openness among many personnel once those walls were lowered, if only in a small way.

So often, while a patient, I felt like I was a teacher, as well. Perhaps Sir Garrod was right; we really are always both teachers and students for each other, no matter what the circumstances.

"Jeff, Dr. Boswell will see you now." I was startled out of my reverie. In an instant, I was once again gripped by fear. The way she said "Dr. Boswell will see you now" had an ominous and sad tone about it. Did she know what was in my file? Was she being particularly nice to show sympathy for what I was about to hear?

The intern entered with a very serious expression on his face. He had my records in his hand. He did know. What was he hiding? "I cannot discuss the results of the tests," he said, "Dr. Boswell will do that." If anything implied the test results were negative, that was it, I thought. Actually, without my knowledge, he was following standard procedure. He checked the stitches on my back and armpit. I was very sweaty and nervous. He asked me a few general questions about my condition, all in a monotone, and then left, saying the doctor would be in shortly to give me the test results. Never in any of my most demanding professional presentations did I experience such apprehension.

After what seemed like an eternity, Dr. Boswell came in, quite expressionless. In a monotone he said, "The results, as I expected were negative." He must have seen a horrified expression on my face, because he looked very startled, and in an instant blurted out, "No Cancer." I felt light-headed, and slipped off the examining table. I vaguely remember giving him a hug and thanking him. Everything after that was a blur until I could get to a phone and call David."

Discussion

Jeff is very much invested in believing the spiritual perspective. He tries to totally embrace the seven principles, which he does intellectually. At the same time, he is dealing with a fear of death, a disbelief that he is his higher self, and that having cancer was his choice. Jeff found that becoming spiritual is a process of accepting and acknowledging he is less spiritual than he desires.

Jeff's intellect saw the spiritual beauty contained within the seven principles. The principle, "We Create and are Responsible for all our Experiences," was self-empowering to him. He wanted to trust this completely. He felt if he could understand why he developed cancer, he would overcome his fears, and prove to himself the beauty and truth of his beliefs.

Jeff cannot tell us which healing method or therapy cured the cancer. It may have been the love and support of his friends, the grieving about his own mortality, the recognition of the influence from a past life, or, simply the surgery itself. Does he know the cancer won't return at a future date? His skin will be monitored for two to three years.

Jeff learned a great deal about himself during this very short, though dramatic, period. Did using the principles and alternative healing methods actually help him heal the cancer? That question is not as readily answered as Jeff would have liked. Using those methods, and adhering to the principles did, however, help release him from the paralyzing fear and helplessness that often accompanies a diagnosis of cancer.

Using the seven principles as a platform provided an opportunity for him to view his situation in a more positive light. He and David were able to develop scenarios around death that allowed for transcendent reflection, learning, and even levity. Being positive freed him from some of the fear. Although he was never fully at peace with cancer, he was able to achieve some comfort through curiosity.

One of the most profound lessons he learned, is that he always had a choice of how to perceive these experiences. At times the fear and sorrow was so great, he could not help taking on the role of a frustrated victim. But, over time, as his curiosity piqued and he surrendered to working with the process, he became increasingly aware of the wisdom of his higher self. Doing this enabled him to learn and grow in ways he could never have anticipated with the limited vision of his conscious mind.

Although there is evidence of sadness and frustration throughout Jeff's account, embracing the possibility that cancer, however life threatening, was part of a larger plan (clearly a manifestation of the third kind), gave him meaning and comfort. Jeff learned to move from the role of victim of a deadly disease, to being self-empowered, with choices in how he viewed his cancer.

Molly's Story

Molly was diagnosed with cancer when she was 29 and told to get her affairs in order because her prognosis was three to five years at the most. Her situation was more grave than Jeff's since her doctor considered her cancer terminal.

I was diagnosed with Hodgkins disease after having a walnut-sized tumor removed from the side of my breast beneath my arm. I bawled for a week, particularly whenever I looked into the faces of my children. My older daughter was 8, my sons 6 and 3, and my younger daughter 11 months old. After a few days of indulging in a major pity party, I decided that I was going to live to see my children grow up and have their own families. I was not going to let those prophets of doom tell me what was going to happen to my life!

I wasn't afraid of dying, due to a near-death experience after a surfing accident when I was nineteen and was left in a coma. I proceeded to the other side after passing through a tunnel and entering brilliant white light. It was beautiful—and so peaceful. I was disappointed when a voice told me it was not my time...I had a lot of work left to do. Because of this experience, I knew within my soul that this lifetime was not all I had before me. However, I did not want to leave my children, and was determined not to.

I had read numerous books on the power of positive thinking, and have always had a very deep belief in God and the power of the universe...even when it wasn't fashionable to do so. I felt I didn't have anything to lose to try and get rid of this Sword of Damocles that was hanging over my head. I thought back to when I had polio as a child, and recalled that I used to picture myself walking normally, even when the doctors said the likelihood was slim. Why wouldn't picturing myself free of cancer work just as well?

Although I didn't know at the time that the technique was called visualization, I imagined the cancerous tendrils shrinking and disappearing, like they had been totally destroyed. I then pictured myself playing with my grandchildren while my grown children stood nearby. I saw myself as a very old woman interacting with my family. I started feeling better after that, both emotionally and physically.

I was scheduled to begin chemotherapy a week before Christmas. I canceled it over the "experts" protests because I refused to be sick from the treatments during the holidays. I finally went in two months later. When the doctor examined me, he couldn't find anything. The signs that the cancer had spread were no longer there. He was puzzled and told me to come back in three months. During the next visit, he told me that they must have made a mistake in the diagnosis, and they labeled the tumor as a non-specific adenitis, which was not totally correct because an 'adenitis' is an inflammatory condition with suppuration...there was no suppuration. But I guess they had to call it something. Anyway that happened 25 years ago and I've never had a recurrence. I now play with my six grandchildren while their parents stand by. Just like in my visualizations.

Maybe I take after my grandmother. In 1948, when Grandma was 75, she was diagnosed with colon cancer. Her age thirtyish doctor told her she had six months to live. She told him she was not ready to go and that she would outlive him. She did. He died during the 1950's, and Grandma passed on in 1974 at the age of 103!

Ann's Story

Ann's skull was fractured when a horse threw her, and she was given a thirty percent chance of survival. When she lived, the doctors gave her an even lower estimate of the likelihood she would ever attain a complete recovery. Through great will and determination she fully recovered. What Ann was unable to share with her doctors was that she had undergone a near death experience during surgery.

———◦•┼•◦———

I floated above my head and looked down on my body in intensive care. I saw people coming in and going out of the room. It was strange seeing my body down below with so much activity around it. It was very peaceful. I looked at my body as a vehicle for getting through this life but it was not me.

I don't actually remember going out of my body. But, in this other dimension there was no light or space or time. It was very loving, very powerful. It was a feeling of love, acceptance, comfort, bliss, joy, knowledge. There was telepathic communication with beings. There was all knowing. There was no need for dialogue. Everything just was. Love was communicated by a feeling. All that was, past, present, future was just there. I experienced all my past lives. There were no boundaries. I knew my soul, and what it had and will experience. I had a sense of my meaning of this existence and my other lives as well. As a soul, I had an understanding of my evolution. I wanted to stay, and I had a choice of staying.

I experienced every being as this massive energy. We were both all connected and separated. We were all a part of the one, and yet I knew I was separate. I now know our connectedness to all things—animals, plants and objects. That is how I see the world now. I knew if I didn't come back in my body now, I would come back some other time. Then, I can remember nestling back into my body. I had made the choice to come back. I knew everything would be all right.

One of the frustrating things was that there was no one to share this experience with. So I kept this incredible happening to myself, even though it was one of the most profound experiences of my life. Fortunately I met people from the manifestation group who encouraged me to share it with them. Now I visit college classes and talk about the experience freely. I feel truly blessed to have had this experience.

Conclusion

Jeff struggled to trust that the higher self was indeed an extension of himself when death seemed to be knocking at his door. He drew on many different types of treatment, including surgical. Sir Garrod never said surgery shouldn't be utilized. In fact, because Jeff's belief system was so comfortable and familiar with this form of treatment, it would have been gravely disadvantageous not to utilize it. But, Jeff did not totally rely on a single method. He utilized all the techniques available to him; from flower essences, to a past life explanation.

What if Jeff had died from the cancer? Would his death have indicated a failure on his part? Not at all, according to Sir Garrod. For some people with cancer, the solution would have been to return to their original state as a spiritual being. There are individuals whose learning may not involve staying in physical form.

McDermott maintains that you cannot automatically assume the most positive outcome of a serious illness or accident is to remain in physical form. It cannot be judged whether learning is best achieved while in physical form, or through returning to the non-physical dimension. One should not place more value on existence in the physical realm than in any other. McDermott said, "So accepting and opening to the divine solution will bring you into a state of peace and to the lesson at hand in that moment without judgment and without failure."

The spiritual plane views death as a transition from the focused state of existence in the physical dimension, to an expanded spiritual state where the individual consciousness merges with its higher self. People such as Ann and Molly, who have had near death experiences, get glimpses of what this process is like. They describe it as a beautiful, wondrous experience filled with love and joy beyond anything we, as humans, can imagine.

From the higher self's broader perspective, the transitions from spirit to physical, and back to spirit, are as mundane as graduating from high school and moving to college, or moving from the single state into the married state. Passing from one state to another represents changes in environmental responsibilities and activities, as one leaves behind old experiences and accepts new challenges and opportunities. From a broader perspective, there is a continuity and meaningfulness in the changes that occur throughout the life cycle.

Graduation or marriage brings a form of death to a previous state, so one can be reborn into a new state of learning and experience. Fellow students or single friends may experience some sadness at the graduation of a peer to the new state, but there is also joy and congratulations as this is recognized as another phase of an ongoing journey.

Do we have to suffer anxiety and pain to complete life's lessons? Perhaps more pleasant ways can be learned. It may be as simple as choosing how we perceive to view our painful experiences. From the point of view of the higher self, curing the cancer seems unimportant, even though it is of primary importance from the point of view of the self. The goal held so dear by a human, is merely a byproduct of the overall process for the higher self.

From Jeff and Molly's limited view points, the anxiety and pain around their cancers were very real. What neither could see was the expanded picture of purpose and learning, of which this particular incarnation occupies only a very small part. Ann's and Molly's near death experiences permitted them to glimpse this beautiful, expanded perspective, if only briefly. Because of it, they will never again fear death.

In the doctor's office, can the very young child who is about to receive a vaccination, appreciate the life-long protection that will follow? All the child knows at that moment, is that the needle is causing a great deal of pain. Given the choice, the child would avoid that pain, just as our ego-based, limited consciousness cannot see the entire master plan lodged within our higher self and would certainly choose to avoid immediate discomfort.

Jeff knew all of this when he was diagnosed with cancer. He was aware death is only a transition. Near death experiences told of a glorious existence on the spiritual plane. He had received useful explanations from Sir Garrod and McDermott about his lessons, which included the influences from a powerful previous incarnation. He embraced many approaches, from traditional to alternative methods, and was surrounded by a large support group of loving individuals. Yet, while waiting in the Doctor's office, he was still afraid.

It seems that in our human state we do have a lot invested in our survival. The fear of annihilation is very powerful, almost instinctual. Jeff did confront those fears; similar to the way Tim confronted the fears surrounding his relationship, and explored the consequences if his worst fears were realized. If he did die, would it really be so bad? Jeff did not fully overcome his fear of death, even with all the support he had. But, for the most part, he did become less fearful over time. His curiosity and powers of observation gave meaning to his cancer even if he did not feel its presence in his life was fully justified. All of the learning he accomplished helped him accept his situation, and this resulted in a greater state of peace. By confronting his fears directly, he moved from a place of obsessive panic to partial acceptance.

We found that whether confronting a disturbing relationship or a life threatening illness, *acceptance* proved to be one of the most valuable resources available in the quest to achieve a measure of comfort and peace.

Chapter 8

CONCLUSION

Acceptance Is a Choice

As we worked with Sir Garrod, Sananda and McDermott over several years, we found ourselves moved from a place of open-minded curiosity and mild skepticism to one of enthusiasm and excitement. We learned that all of life's experiences had a purpose, even if much of the understanding was beyond our consciousness. Because we chose many of our experiences from beyond our conscious awareness and were responsible for everything in our lives, we created what we called "manifestations of the third kind."

The seven principles emerged from the massive amount of information we gleaned from the channeled entities, and served to organize their central explanations of our spiritual heritage. The principles provided a useful framework to discuss this knowledge. We are spiritual beings inhabiting physical bodies so that we may have experiences we could not undergo in our spiritual state.

The channeled entities helped us understand why we had experiences that we neither consciously desired, nor did they seem to originate in our subconscious beliefs. They told us that we each designed a set of lessons, and selected the path to learn them before we were even born. After birth, we attract experiences and people into our lives to help us learn those lessons. Those whom we attract usually have their own lessons to explore. It is a mutually cooperative venture. In addition, there are still larger lessons of a cooperative nature which involve families, groups, and whole societies.

We always retain the choice of whether to learn our lessons or ignore them. If we can reach the inner part of us connected to the superconscious which is cognizant of our particular plan, we find we can comprehend more of the events manifesting in our lives, and why we are undergoing them. We can then more consciously choose how, or if, we wish to respond to the events we are attracting to ourselves.

As we learned more during our discussions with Sir Garrod, Sananda and McDermott, we found the spiritual perspective which advocated self responsibility, was compelling, not only for adding new insight into our personal lives, but also for providing answers to some of the major societal issues (such as war, poverty, and crime) that concerned us. We were told, as we healed and empowered ourselves, we also assist in healing and empowering others; those we personally interact with, and through the principle of interconnectedness of all matter, the entire world community—even the planet itself.

If we believe we create all of our experiences to facilitate personal growth and learning, there is no need to blame others for the problems we are experiencing in our own lives. As we heal our own personal angers and fears, there will be no need for war, poverty, or crime, since they are basically collective projections of everyone's fears. McDermott reminded us, "If everyone believed that they could create anything they needed, it would follow that no one would blame anyone else, or take from anyone else, because we would know we could create what we needed. And, we would not need to seek retribution from someone if they took something, believing they could not create it for themselves, because we would know we could recreate it. The truth is, there is infinite abundance of everything you need and everything you could possibly want."

These perspectives were so beautiful, and so intriguing, we wanted to totally embrace them. To do so was difficult for us because these principles were so different from the values and beliefs we had lived with for most of our lives. Our culture supports a belief that authority, expertise, and responsibility lay outside the self. As a result, it is hard to accept that major physical disability, criminal acts, car accidents, or environmental disasters are the products of choices we made.

Intellectually, this concept involved a major shift in perspective. How could we really know we had created everything in our lives, and were responsible for our own growth and learning? We wanted proof before we were willing to embrace this new set of beliefs. We wanted to believe in this inviting new concept, but first, we needed to understand how it worked in our lives. Before we would *trust* these new principles, we wanted to test them out.

Both of us were well trained in the scientific method, and were open to a demonstration of the validity of this information about our spiritual nature. Although we might not admit it, understanding how these principles worked in our lives would give us a sense of mastery over this process. It seemed natural to think if we could understand something, we could exercise some control over it. We feel vulnerable and helpless when we don't know what is effecting us, particularly if it is something we want to change. Often, our greatest fear is the fear of the unknown. Usually the first step to changing an undesirable situation, or healing discomfort, is to identify the cause of that problem. This type of awareness implies the possibility of control.

We did feel confident with some of the spiritual messages. Already, there was an abundance of evidence confirming the principle of the interconnectedness of matter. All of our previous work surrounding manifestations of the first and second kinds supported this. Other published scientific research linking consciousness and matter also reinforced this principle. A substantial amount of material in the field of quantum physics on the study of subatomic particles appeared consistent with what we were learning from Sir Garrod, McDermott, and Sananda.

Regarding the principle that all experiences we attract into our lives are for our learning and growth, we were often able to uncover explanations and patterns that helped provide insight for experiences in our lives. Barbara, for example, was able to interpret her many job experiences as not only leading her toward a very satisfying career, but also serving to build her confidence, and helping her learn to trust her inner guidance. Mark, who sought a romantic relationship, was able to see a pattern of less-than-satisfying liaisons progressing into less-stressful, healthier relationships as he learned valuable lessons and healed issues within himself.

In most cases, we could only see the patterns, and derive some understanding of the situations and people we were attracting into our lives, well after the fact. We both marveled at how we had ended up meeting each other through an association with the same channeled entity, and the same energy healer, while seeking relief from an identical physical ailment. Such incidents were too perfect to be coincidental, particularly when supported by many other such occurrences of our own and others in the manifestation group.

Although uncovering the meaning of our experiences was easier to do in retrospect, we asked whether it was possible to discover the reasons why things happen as the events unfolded.

For example, the knowledge might ease the fear and anxiety caused by being fired from a job, if it were possible to recognize that the unpleasant event was part of one's life plan and was destined to open the way to more challenging and enjoyable employment. It is easier to accept an unpleasant event if it is known to be part of, or in the service of, a higher cause.

Understanding in the moment is unusual, such as the problem Jim encountered with the car hood. When the incident occurred, at first Jim was as frustrated as any of us would be. He had a well-orchestrated meeting arranged, which required coordinating different people from several locations. It is very understandable that he was not happy with his circumstances. However, although Jim never stood on the side of the road reflecting on all the opportunities for learning his higher self was presenting to him, he did have a conscious awareness that something more than his immediate crisis was unfolding. He knew he had a choice; he could resist what was happening, or he could choose to "go with it," and trust that the meeting would work out. As he told us later, "This horse wasn't going where I wanted it to go, so I decided I would go with it in the direction it was going."

As we continued to work with our own life experiences, and those of others, it became clear to us that not only was it difficult to access information about situations as they were occurring, but often the information we were given was fragmentary. We were dealing with a multidimensional phenomena, with lessons that went far beyond what we could ever comprehend, much less validate.

Those fragmentary explanations were far from unimportant, however. If we were struck by an unpleasant or catastrophic event, we at least wanted some justification for our discomfort. We felt automatically trusting that our higher selves were experiencing learning or growth, was too much to expect. The fragments provided insight for us.

For Jeff, who had cancer, there was an internal feeling, a sense of correctness, when Sir Garrod and McDermott told him he was healing issues around his physical body, derived not only from this life, but also from issues during a past life when he lived as a very self-righteous Catholic priest. However, while it was useful information, it didn't completely convince Jeff. He wasn't sure it was enough to justify having cancer, and Jeff needed to justify the cancer in order to accept it.

We received glimpses, bits and scraps of interpretation, but we were not capable of understanding the whole picture. McDermott pointed out that each individual is a significant evolving jewel in a vast intricate web, cooperatively linked with other organically evolving interconnected jewels, infinite in number, and existing on many levels, in numerous different dimensions of reality. If this were not enough, they told us time and space is also an illusion. The latter was definitely way beyond our comprehension.

Still, these fragments of interpretations were very helpful to us as we developed a sense of trust and acceptance in what was unfolding in our daily lives. We were learning how events, when viewed in retrospect, were part of a positive learning process, and often brought to us what we consciously desired. This past history of information made it easier to trust the inexplicable events we encountered.

For Mark, seeing how his past relationships had brought him valuable healing and learning which guided him toward the direction he wanted to go, made it easier for him to trust in the moment in his present relationship. In the moment, he could not see where this was leading, but he trusted, based on prior experience, that there was a higher purpose, and, at the very least, fragments of meaning and understanding would be revealed over time. He was finally able to see that the process contained a purpose, in contrast to his previous viewpoint, in which he believed he was a failure if he did not get the relationship desired.

While understanding our past experiences did help us trust in unexplained circumstances in the present, we were also aware we were not seeing the big picture. Some events seemed logical, sensible, and consistent with what we were experiencing, while others questioned our beliefs and were not open to ordinary means of validation.

We also found that understanding an event, and using the seven principles when working through its challenges, did not eliminate the very human reactions of fear and frustration that often accompany inexplicable events. Jeff's fear of death was only partially ameliorated with the comfort offered by the principles, and the support of a friend.

However, even though the seven principles only offered partial understandings and partial comfort, we did find the seventh principle one of the most important. Whether we had enough knowledge to avoid or change a situation, or whether or not we had a reasonable explanation for an event, we still had another option of how we wished to view our experiences.

The knowledge that we could *accept* a situation did not become apparent to us until after we considered other options (change, avoidance, or a verifiable explanation), and found them ineffective, and/or inadequate. To accept whatever was happening in the moment, meant to have no anticipation or expectation around the situation's potential consequences.

Until then, we had never realized that acceptance was actually a *choice*. In fact, we had thought that to accept, to surrender to a situation, was equivalent to admitting failure. It was only after we had exhausted all other options that we considered acceptance.

At that point, acceptance was a real choice, taking its place among other available options. It was one more way we could *choose* to perceive our experiences. We found that this action, in certain circumstances, turned out to be very positive, and, in some cases, transformative.

Ironically, by choosing acceptance and giving up trying to control, we gained control.

We knew from our work with the manifestation concept, that if we interpreted present experiences positively, this positive energy tended to create still more positive outcomes. The reverse was the case if we chose to perceive situations negatively. We learned that our less-conscious beliefs or manifestations of the second kind were powerful expressions in our daily lives. If we had a positive outlook on life, positive events and outcomes were more common.

But, we were not always able to come up with significant positive interpretations, particularly in the short term. When Jeff was told he had cancer, he found it very difficult, at least at first, to discover what was positive about his condition. He also found it difficult to deny its presence. Resisting or denying an unpleasant circumstance can serve to attract more of the same, however, it may be difficult to be sufficiently detached to find a positive explanation for the undesirable situation. It is in those circumstances that acceptance becomes a meaningful and self-affirming choice. Those who are uncomfortable with the principle of self-responsibility, particularly for a life-threatening situation, may feel more comfortable with a belief that the outcome of their condition is in God's hands.

For Jeff, because of a strong need to find a cause for, or at least an understanding of, his illness so he could exercise control over its outcome, acceptance was easier after he found justification. Because Mark was able to see how all the relationships he had attracted into his life were meaningful, and on a path to his desired relationship, it was easier for him to trust, and not judge, the presence of more recent relationships.

When Bill tried to save his marriage, he visualized all the choices available to him. But, after considering these possibilities, he chose acceptance. As a result, the option he resisted the most, turned out to be the best. He saw how the alternatives would not have served him in the long run. He did not want his wife to remain in their relationship because she was forced to be with him. Control mechanisms never work, although they may for a short time. He surrendered control to his higher self, and accepted his wife and her needs. He accepted what was happening in the present, and whatever would happen in the future. When he accepted and surrendered to the situation's natural evolution, it didn't mean he did not wish a positive result. Bill recognized it was not necessary for his wife to change in order to get what he wanted. In fact, it was possible that for him to get what he wanted in a relationship, he might have to consider divorce as a first step.

Interestingly enough, by accepting, the situation transformed. Even if the relationship had dissolved, by definition through acceptance, it would no longer be a problem. Through acceptance, Bill survived his greatest fears.

Detaching from outcome and allowing for possibilities is a very powerful tool as Tom demonstrated when his asthma almost totally disappeared while he was focused on pending surgery or writing poetry. When we resist unpleasantness by focusing so much energy on trying to make something happen, we actually give energy to its negativity and contribute to its presence. If Tom were to fully accept his asthma in an act of self love, it could disappear, or, at least, no longer be an issue. In any case, if he accepted the asthma's presence, it would cease to be a problem. When you accept, you are authorized to have the problem, and the problem frequently dissipates.

It is possible to go right to acceptance, rather than build up a sense of trust through a history of understandings, as did Jeff. It can also be accomplished through considering a wide range of choices, as Bill demonstrated. More and more, we found it to be true, particularly around dramatic events. It is not necessary to go through a list of options, or try to understand everything, in order to accept.

Another way to reach acceptance is to clearly recognize and *acknowledge* where you are in the moment. You may be in a state of non-acceptance. At times it is very natural to go through a period of non-acceptance in order to arrive at a place of acceptance. Mary, possessing a considerable awareness of the spiritual principles, initially chose to react to the breakup of her relationship with frustration and anger. She chose to be the victim of an insensitive and unfaithful lover. Accepting where she was in the moment (a place of anger and blame) was honest, and allowed her to heal her disappointment much more rapidly than if she had denied her true feelings. Resisting her feelings would probably have intensified them, and hindered the understanding that followed. Knowledge of the lessons and the learning accomplished would emerge at a later point when she was ready to accept them.

We have found that by accepting our feelings, including anger and disappointment, it is possible to have an awareness of what we are doing during, or very soon after, the incident. An example is the immediate frustration Jim felt when the hood of his car unlatched. We are human beings, with human reactions learned over many years of socialization. There are times we want to be victims. Unfortunately, denying the presence of these feelings and attitudes only gives them more power over us.

In conclusion, in all our work with the seven principles, we learned it is especially helpful for us to be easy on ourselves. Although there is nothing magical about the principles or their number, they provide a useful framework for discussion and give us a helpful resource from which to view the day-to-day events in our lives.

Through researching these concepts, we now realize how many more options are available to us when we encounter the events in our lives than we anticipated before this project was initiated. While we now have a framework with which to play detective while exploring and interpreting the purpose behind the situations attracted into our lives, we also have built a firmer foundation for trust and acceptance, even when understanding and justification are absent. The awareness and application of both seeking purpose for, and surrendering to, the immediate situation has resulted in our lives running more smoothly, being more peaceful, and, finally, becoming more interesting and enjoyable.

Discovering the principle of acceptance as a choice was one of the most significant revelations of this whole project. We learned that acceptance came from a place of power and authority, while resignation came from a place of weakness and submission. Change, paradoxically, usually came from a place of allowance and surrender.

When we accepted what was in the moment, we disconnected from any anticipated consequence, no matter how firmly it seemed connected to the present situation. We learned that, at best, we only see fragments of a much larger picture; similar to seeing only one scene out of an entire movie. What we know is often based on our past experiences, which influence the choices we make, and frequently serve to limit the possibilities that may unfold in our future. McDermott reminds us, "When you come through the mind, you are using the most limited part of your consciousness to guide you. The mind could convince you that a minefield of explosives was a flower garden." Conversely, when we accept the moment, and allow and listen for guidance, we intuitively expand our possibilities. To trust without any conscious understanding is an affirming and powerful choice.

EPILOGUE

Acceptance Is a Challenge

As we go into our second printing of *Manifesting Your Heart's Desire Book II,* some five years have passed. The significance of individual "choice" is still central to our thinking. Our intent has been to present an alternative to the "self as victim" perspective so widespread in our society today. Faced with the challenges of our life today, it is tempting to make someone else responsible for our troubles and perceived failures. Better to blame someone outside yourself, a parent, a spouse, the government, society, even God, than to accept responsibility yourself.

This "victim" approach disempowers us, as it mandates that someone, or something, outside of ourselves must change before our own circumstances can change. The alternative is to embrace the process of manifesting in which we are the creators of our lives, and assume responsibility for what we have created. In doing so, we reclaim the power to change our circumstances, and thus our lives, to something more desirable.

It is perhaps most difficult to accept our personal circumstances during times of crises or immediate need. These situations are also the most difficult for us to "detach" from the outcome. It is easy to "let go" of a desired parking place. It is not easy to trust the unfolding of a desired outcome if it involves a life-threatening illness, or to be patient when we have no job or are lonely for a partner.

To accept such situations more easily, it helps to view life's circumstances from a more expanded spiritual perspective. These "manifestations of a third kind" seem to exist outside our consciousness. Their origin lies in an expanded part of our consciousness, our Higher Self. After we incarnate in human form, we draw to ourselves those individuals, experiences and situations that facilitate our growth.

Even though the broad lessons have already been chosen before we incarnate, we have considerable latitude in how, or even if, we learn those lessons that further our growth. We can learn them with a great deal of drama or learn them quite simply. Our intuition can assist us in navigating through these circumstances, and help us understand the lessons they are presenting to us.

Revisiting some of the cases previously discussed illustrates the nature of manifestation as a continuous process, a process with styles unique to each individual.. Mary who was learning how to be less needy in her relationships claims she has finally realized her manifestation of ten years. Her partner turned out to be her best friend and, as she reports, "under my nose" all the time. "We just had to get to the right point in our own growth separately, before we could do that growth together. I've never known such joy and happiness." Mary has learned to become more comfortable with the process, and to be less attached to the outcome or goal.

Mark, who was learning to trust his "heart" and place less emphasis on his "head" met his partner, married and reports that he has never been happier. He said that when he placed less reliance on his rational list of traits, and more on what he was feeling, he was successful in attaining his goal. "I simply spent some time each day imagining what it would be like to be with her. How I would feel while she was with me. The closeness, the sharing, the intimacy was all part of my vision and fantasy experience. It was fun just spending time in that state. "

His future wife, Tracy, also manifested a relationship. Her technique was to write daily in a gratitude journal and to recognize the power of trust in a higher power. She also had a list of traits she wanted in a relationship but she believed her success was in her ability to trust the universe "to set things in motion and to make it happen."

Several months later, after finally meeting Mark, she wrote, "it is far better than I had imagined. The key is to trust your higher self to bring you the right partner at the right time. It is when we truly give up and accept whatever manifests, that the desired relationship appears. It is so freeing to say 'It's in your hands. I completely trust your judgment to bring the next right thing into my life. And then it occurred like a miracle unfolding!"

For Tracy this strong belief and trust that her higher self would manifest her desire at the right time allowed her to be patient and let the universe to do its work. Although putting less emphasis on the list of traits she desired in a partner, she did get most of the traits on her list. The Universe had provided a wonderfully perfect solution for her.

For Mark, this comfort and acceptance came from the gradual awareness and appreciation of all the various lessons he was learning along the way. Each relationship had something to offer him, and he could feel himself growing in confidence and understanding as his process unfolded.

The nature of manifestation as a continuous process can also be seen in situations involving healing. Tom learned to listen to his inner voice in seeking a cure for his asthma. His asthma and allergies have actually declined about 80% and his quality of life has improved dramatically. He has become less and less dependent on conventional medicine while his confidence in his own ability to heal has grown substantially. He has done an excellent job working with and stretching his belief system.

It is tempting to only share the stories that result in successful outcomes. However, we feel we would be remiss if we did not report the cases of those who made remarkable progress but had not experienced total "success". The results may be less spectacular, but for the asthma patient, for example, the improvement in health has been incredible and he is very grateful for his improved health. We suspect his perspective of expressing gratitude will continue to create an even higher state of health for him in the future.

A similar outcome of improvement without total success typifies Jeff's situation. Over the years he has created a supportive environment so that his melanomas have been caught earlier, and the surgical procedures and the stress accompanying them reduced considerably. This appeals to Jeff who likes to exercise a lot of control in his life. He has been learning how to live with cancer and not to fear it. He does not know why he has not totally healed all possibility of cancer. Perhaps he is still learning to be more loving and accepting of his physical body even with its perceived flaws. And he recognizes his personal lessons may also be part of larger group lessons associated with the global environment.

As we reflect back over the past five years, we basically re-affirm our belief in "acceptance as a choice", but also add that this desired state of "acceptance" is not always that easy to attain. The path we take to achieve acceptance is a very individual process. We recognize that the understanding we come to about a particular life experience is probably very incomplete and fragmentary from the perspective of the Higher Self. Yet, it was still helpful for many of the group members to find some meaning, however incomplete it might be, into what they were experiencing. Some could see a pattern to their experiences and learn from them. And, in that seeing, they experienced a very welcome feeling of comfort and control.

Others could not perceive a pattern and instead chose to use an approach of basic trust and "flow" in the outcome. This trust approach is particularly helpful when faced with our most challenging experiences such as accident, ill health and personal relationships. In choosing this approach, it is easier to embrace the concept that we choose and create everything in our life. We believe that we will, in time, understand the value of the present situation and its lesson for our life's learning and growth. This belief then provides the bridge we need to accept what we are now experiencing in all it's fullness and richness. The Universe does truly bless us!

AFTERWORD

Understanding how the process of manifestation operates in our daily lives is an ongoing exploration. This is the second book in this series. We are looking to write a third book, again derived from group personal experiences.

If you are interested in learning more about Manifesting, you can find us on the World Wide Web at:

http://www.uvm.edu/~afengler/

This site serves as a way to provide information and stories about manifesting to interested readers as well as permitting questions and comments to be addressed directly to the authors. Visiting the site can facilitate networking with like minded people and also provide information about additional materials related to the subject of manifestation.

Many readers are forming manifesting support groups. It's a great way to grow and expand our beliefs. More information about support groups can be found on our Web site.

CPSIA information can be obtained at www.ICGtesting.com
Printed in the USA
BVOW08s0958210915

418919BV00001B/89/P